To my ... John ~~Milner~~ with affection

THE EPISCOPAL CHURCH

Its Message for Men of Today

BY

GEORGE PARKIN ATWATER
RECTOR OF THE
CHURCH OF OUR SAVIOUR
AKRON, OHIO

THE MOREHOUSE PUBLISHING CO.
MILWAUKEE, WISCONSIN

Copyright, 1917
By
George Parkin Atwater

Printing Statement:

Due to the very old age and scarcity of this book, many of the pages may be hard to read due to the blurring of the original text, possible missing pages, missing text, dark backgrounds and other issues beyond our control.

Because this is such an important and rare work, we believe it is best to reproduce this book regardless of its original condition.

Thank you for your understanding.

TO THE FAITHFUL PEOPLE
OF
THE CHURCH OF OUR SAVIOUR
AKRON, OHIO
WITH WHOM HE HAS SERVED
THE TWENTY YEARS OF HIS MINISTRY
THIS BOOK
IS AFFECTIONATELY DEDICATED
BY THEIR RECTOR

"No complex or very important truth was ever transferred in full development from one mind to another; truth of that character is not a piece of furniture to be shifted; it is a seed which must be sown, and pass through the several stages of growth. No doctrine of importance can be transferred in a matured shape into any man's understanding from without: it must arise by an act of genesis within the understanding itself."

—*De Quincey.*

Contents

		Page
I.	THE CHURCH AND PUBLIC WORSHIP	1
II.	THE ACTIVE WORSHIP OF THE PEOPLE	18
III.	THE PRAYER BOOK AND PUBLIC WORSHIP	32
IV.	BAPTISM AND CHURCH MEMBERSHIP	48
V.	THE APOSTLES' CREED	63
VI.	THE HOLY COMMUNION	82
VII.	THE HISTORIC MINISTRY	97
VIII.	THE HISTORY OF THE CHURCH	110
IX.	THE BACKGROUND OF WORSHIP	124
X.	THE CHRISTIAN YEAR	138
XI.	THE CHURCH AND MEN OF TODAY	153
XII.	THE APPEAL OF RELIGION TO MEN	169

PREFACE

These apparent obstacles are, I am convinced, the result of misunderstanding and of the lack of definite information. When the Church is seen as a whole; when its purpose in its services is fully made known; when its reasons for its methods are made clear, the obstacles vanish.

It is quite certain, as experience has taught many a minister of the Church, that there are many people who are adrift from religious affiliation because they believe they cannot conform to the practices, or fulfill the expectations, of church membership. To such the Episcopal Church has a message of deepest import. The Church presents a teaching and practice, which, when understood, have claimed the enthusiastic allegiance of many who have felt an uncomfortable isolation from religious associations. The faith of the Episcopal Church is sane, reasonable, and of right proportions. Its practices are stimulating and satisfying and strengthening. Its methods are calm and healing. It has an atmosphere of joy and peace. Its purpose is to educate the people in the life of the Kingdom of God, and to do this with care, patience and with sympathy. The Church is not exclusive, but inclusive of every soul having a good intention. It is not the judge and the accuser of its people but their advocate and friend.

This book is intended for those who would understand the Episcopal Church; both its spirit and practices. It considers chiefly the initial difficulties of those coming for the first time within the influence of the Church. It is not a manual of Christian doctrine, or a complete exposition of the Church. There are many such manuals, which should be read by any who wish a full statement.

To those who desire to gain a better knowledge of the Episcopal Church, I venture to offer a suggestion. Attend, for a time, the services of the Church with an effort to understand them. No great spiritual forces in actual operation can be understood and appreciated by study alone, without the corrective and broadening influences of experience in contact with those forces. A great book must be read to be appreciated. The critics can never give an adequate presentation of its charm and power. Appreciation of the Church is likewise a matter of experience. It is certainly worth time and effort to gain some knowledge of the Mother Church of the English speaking people. The services are not so involved as many imagine. An hour's careful examination of the Prayer Book will make them plain. The Prayer Book itself should be in every home. Next to the Bible it has been the book of greatest influence in moulding the religious life of our race.

The Church always welcomes the inquirer, and its ministers are ready to give him instruc-

PREFACE

tion. The Church likewise asks no repudiation or distrust of one's previous Christian experience. But with its greater experience, extending through many generations, corrected and enriched by its comprehensive contact with multitudes of lives, the Church supplements and enlarges the religious training of those who come within its portals.

This book is intended to create a favorable opinion of the Church, by an expression of what the writer believes to be its true spirit toward its people. Nor are these words written in the seclusion of an academic cloister, but in the study of one who for twenty years has been talking with men and women about these subjects.

May I explain the literary form into which these simple talks are cast? I have adopted this method of a conversation among friends because it permits of more flexible presentation of the subject. It is the natural method of the teacher. Every statement has been as carefully weighed, however, as if it were part of a treatise.

My only hope in presenting this book is that it will not be understood as a complete treatise but that it will help to remove the apparent obstacles in the minds of those to whom the Episcopal Church is extending a welcome.

GEORGE PARKIN ATWATER.

MARVIN PARISH HOUSE
ST. ANDREW'S DAY
AKRON, OHIO
1917

THE EPISCOPAL CHURCH

ITS MESSAGE FOR MEN OF TODAY

CHAPTER I.

THE CHURCH AND PUBLIC WORSHIP.

"WELL, Rector," exclaimed the Doctor, as he stood before the fire in the Rector's study, "I went to church last Sunday."

This was not exactly news, for the Rector had noticed him there and was prepared for a discussion of the event.

"Bravo!" called out the Judge, who as Senior Warden of the parish occupied the most comfortable chair. "Hear that, Major," addressing the fourth man present who was glancing at the books which lined the walls.

"I saw him there," replied the Major without looking around. "Didn't hurt you a bit, did it, Doctor?" he asked quietly as he took down a rather worn volume entitled "Fishing as a Fine Art."

The Doctor laughed. "Temperature normal, heart action regular," he replied.

The Rector kept quiet for the moment. These four men were warm friends who often gathered in the Rector's study to enjoy each other's company and to discuss the score of things that interest men. The Judge was a sturdy Churchman, loyal, and ever thoughtful for the Church's good. The Major was an alert, practical man, with a tendency to judge methods by results. The Doctor was a keen man of exact training, with a respect for religion, but with little knowledge of it except remnants of early memories in a rather rigid congregation.

"Had you ever attended an Episcopal Church before?" finally asked the Rector.

"Never," answered the Doctor cheerfully. "It was a new experience. I have been to plenty of others," he added, as if defending himself against a charge of total neglect.

"Now, Doctor," continued the Judge with a more serious inflection in his voice, "You have a chance to make a real contribution to our fund of knowledge. I should like very much to know the impressions of a mature man in his first attendance at a service of the Episcopal Church."

The Doctor hesitated a moment. "It is not exactly as if I had a novel experience," he explained, "because I have had some idea of what to expect and likewise I have had some notions, perhaps you may call them prejudices, about the Episcopal Church. They are, perhaps, not founded on reliable information but they seem to prevail among persons like myself who have been reared in a different atmosphere. These came to mind during the service."

"Did the service, and your impression of it, confirm your notions?" asked the Major, putting down his book and drawing up a chair to the fireside.

"Not exactly," replied the Doctor, "but, at the same time, the notions were not entirely banished."

"Suppose you tell us your impressions," suggested the Rector, "both the favorable and the unfavorable ones, and then later let us take stock of the notions."

The Doctor laughed. "Is this a conspiracy to make me unburden my rather meagre knowledge of religion?" he asked.

"Not at all, Doctor," declared the Judge, "but I am under the impression that we who are accustomed to the Church do not fully realize the difficulties that confront those who come to the Church for the first time. A frank statement from you would give us an idea of what we ought to do to make the practices of the Church clear."

"In that case," answered the Doctor, "I shall be frank. I am inclined on general grounds to like the Church, but it is difficult for me to understand it entirely. I went last Sunday with good intentions. As soon as I entered and had been in the pew for a few minutes I realized that the atmosphere was different from many a church I had attended. The people who entered early did not sit and talk with each other. They were reverent. That impressed me very much, and favorably."

"They were in the House of God," said the Judge simply. "We never use the church for any purpose except the services, and our people are accustomed to reverence. It is the Temple of God twenty-four hours a day and whenever one enters it he feels that it is devoted to a sacred purpose."

"The attitude of the congregation clearly indicated that," was the Doctor's comment. "I noticed, too, that most of the people kneeled a moment in prayer when they entered the pews. That made me somewhat uncomfortable for I had not done so and I didn't want to seem conspicuous."

"Just a moment," interrupted the Rector. "I wish to make the emphatic statement that the

Church welcomes visitors, strangers, and newcomers, to our services. We are glad to have them come. They may take part in the service, or not, just as they wish. They may stand and kneel, or not, as they wish. They need not feel conspicuous, as our people understand the situation fully. They need not feel embarrassed. Probably most of the people in the church have been new-comers at some time and they sympathize with the initial difficulties of the stranger. Come on your own terms, Doctor."

"Well, that is certainly satisfactory and I'll feel better next time."

"You see, we old timers," added the Judge, "find the habits of the Church second nature, but we want people to come because we respect them, and not because of their habits of worship."

"Why did the people kneel?" asked the Doctor directly.

"To prepare their minds for the service," replied the Rector, "and to ask a blessing upon all who are to take part in it."

"To try to disconnect their thoughts from automobiles, golf hazards, and Sunday dinner," added the Major in a low voice.

The Rector laughed. The Major was accustomed to state things in a blunt way. It was good to hear a layman's frank statement. It seemed to take a certain unreality from the discussion of religious things.

"Good idea," added the Doctor. "After that my impressions were more general. The next thing that struck me was that you didn't sing meaningless hymns. I read one or two. They are good poetry, even without music."

"The best the market affords," commented the Major drily. "Too many good hymns to waste time on the poor ones. Religion has ever been indebted to inspiring music."

"There were some other good impressions," admitted the Doctor candidly. "But on the whole I failed to see the general trend of it all. To be perfectly frank I was in the presence of a public worship that was cloudy. In the first place I did not understand why you wore vestments, and why the choir wore vestments; why there was so much standing and kneeling, why you had so many colored hangings about, why you read so much out of your Prayer Book and indeed why you use a Prayer Book at all. It looked to me like a complicated way to worship, with more attention paid to forms than to the real purpose of the occasion."

"That brings us to the fundamentals, Doctor," replied the Rector. "If you will permit, let us pass by the particular things for a moment and try to understand the principles that govern the methods of our worship."

"That's getting to fundamentals," commented the Major, settling back to listen. "No sermon, however," he cautioned.

"Plain common sense, I hope," the Rector assured him. "To understand the public worship of the Episcopal Church, you must grasp three principles. They will serve to interpret practically all of its practices and habits. You may not approve of these principles but at any rate you can understand that the Church has reason for adhering to them. These principles of the Church are the basis of its practices.

"The first principle is that the Church attempts to appeal to the eye as well as to the ear."

"Modern educational method," put in the Major. "Visit a school room today. Pictures, maps, charts, cubes, squares, and diagrams. Flowers too."

"The eye is one of the gateways of knowledge," continued the Rector. "Many of our great arts are appeals to the eye. All architecture and painting are addressed to the eye. The Church has for a thousand years or more attempted to instruct the people by education through the eye.

"For that reason our churches are furnished so that each great function of the Church has some article of furniture which constantly suggests that function. Why did you hang out a flag before your office last Fourth of July?" questioned the Rector.

"Patriotic," said the Doctor, smiling.

"An appeal to the eye," declared the Rector. "The flag has no voice, and no words are on it. Yet it speaks and proclaims love of country and loyalty. Every time we see the flag it stirs us with the thought that our fathers died for it, and that we are to live for it, and to die for it, if necessary. The flag is a great teacher.

"So the Church erects an Altar in the most conspicuous place in the chancel to remind the people constantly that what takes place at the Altar is a service of Christ's own institution. We place a cross upon the Altar to remind them, and indeed to teach them, that Christ died upon the cross for the sins of the whole world. It is our flag."

"I can see that," admitted the Doctor, "but why the flowers and the candles? Are they mere decorations?"

"Not at all. The flowers symbolize the joy of religion. Some people think that religious services are gloomy and joyless. Too many people get their impression of the main emphasis of religion from funerals. They think that religion is to teach men how to die. Inasmuch as you are healthy it does not appeal particularly. But religion is to teach one how to live. Life should be filled with joy."

"But my garden may teach me that," suggested the Doctor.

"True. But the flowers, on the Altar beside the Cross, are to teach that the joy of life is closely connected with the fact that Christ died for men.

"So too the candles. They teach that Christ is the light of the world in His human and divine natures. Our religion is not darkness but light. It lights our pathway."

"I think I see," said the Doctor seriously. "Your Altar then is like a great picture which sets forth the religious teachings of the Church."

"Exactly," affirmed the Rector. "It is a teaching picture. But it is more than that. The service of the Altar is intended to bring the Power of the Cross, the Joy symbolized in the flowers, and the Light, symbolized by the candles, into the lives of men."

"I thought the sermon did that," was the Doctor's comment.

"The sermon instructs, interprets, stimulates—" began the Rector.

"If it is not too long," commented the Major with a glance at the Rector.

"Exactly," asserted the Rector. "We need more than the sermon however. We need variety of impression to maintain attention. The Church teaches when men are silent."

"Did you ever go, alone, into an Episcopal Church?" asked the Judge.

"No, I think not. Why should I?" asked the Doctor.

"It would be a good experience," replied the Judge. "The peculiar thing about it is that it never seems *empty*. I have sometimes sat for half an hour in our church to allow the church to teach me. Somehow the absence of people does not make the church seem lonely or bare. The Altar seems to stir up memories and resolutions. The whole effect is as a voice speaking to the soul. There is no actual sound, but one seems to be listening to a great organ played by some invisible organist. In the midst of the rush and turmoil of this day every man would find it a valuable practice to spend an occasional half hour in our church and recall to himself the deeper duties of life."

"And think on his sins," added the Major.

"Quite so," said the Judge, "especially when we find the world ready to encourage our sins."

The Doctor was clearly impressed. "I thought churches were for public gatherings," he said quietly.

"They are," agreed the Judge, "but they are likewise for individual edification. The mistake you may make about the Episcopal Church is in thinking that it is an organization having as its object public assemblies, in which a general effort is made to promote goodness. It is more than that. It is a great Mother who teaches you so impressively that its influence and control endure throughout the week. The idea of righteousness and the idea of salvation are often too abstract. The Church is the embodiment of these ideas. You know the spirit of college?" asked the Judge.

"Class of 1905," said the Doctor. "Best college on earth."

"That's loyalty," affirmed the Judge. "The college stands for education. Its activities tend toward the development of the student. It expresses great ideas and trains men in a score of ways. Do you keep your old text-books?"

"Shelf full of them," confessed the Doctor.

"Pretty dry now, aren't they?" questioned the Judge. "Yet they have the heart of the substance of your education in them. But it was the college that made those books live. You were part of all that. So the Church is a great living organization to which loyalty and love and devotion respond. You are proud of it, and you carry the thought of it with you constantly. On days when services are held the people come to pledge anew their faith, to refresh their devotion, to learn more, and to quicken their spiritual life. They come not as chance spectators of a service, or accidental listeners to a moral lecture, but as part of the whole body of the Church."

"That's a fine ideal," admitted the Doctor, "but the Church never impressed me in that way."

"You have misunderstood it," said the Judge simply. "It is our spiritual home. So we keep it orderly and furnish it gloriously. We like that picture of the Altar and the Cross, even as you like the warmth and glow of your hearthstone. The hearthstone has symbolized all that is lovely and enduring in the life of the family, its joys as well as its duties."

"And does that explain the other features of your church furnishings?" asked the Doctor.

"It does. The Judge has exactly expressed it," said the Rector. "We furnish the Church for instruction, for usefulness, and for the general atmosphere. We have a Font, near the entrance, to symbolize the fact that Baptism is the entrance to the Household of God. The Pulpit indicates the teaching and preaching functions. The Lectern, on which rests the Bible, indicates the reverence paid to the Bible. And the prayer desk and choir stalls are for the ministry of prayer and praise."

"That brings me to another question," said the Doctor. "Why do the minister and choir wear vestments?"

Both the Rector and the Major began to reply.

"To show their ministry of prayer and praise," began the Rector.

"Democratic!" urged the Major.

"That brings us to the second underlying principle of the Church," interrupted the Rector. "The Episcopal Church is democratic. The world over it serves all sorts and conditions of men. It has the same services and ministers in the same way to rich and poor, fortunate and unfortunate. It brings the universal spiritual satisfactions to the universal needs of our common human nature."

"But how are vested choirs democratic?" asked the Doctor.

"Nothing so democratic as a uniform," answered the Major. "Variety in uniform shows distinctive duties, but all uniforms are democratic. One minister is not clothed in fine broadcloth and another in homespun. All wear the simple vestments of their rank. Choristers too! Many a person would be kept out of a choir by lack of proper clothes if choirs were not in uniform. Nothing so distracting as a mixed choir in a denominational church. Twenty different kinds of hats, as many kinds of cravats. Whole scheme of unvested choirs too formal and aristocratic. Our method much simpler and democratic. Admits persons who would be excluded if fine clothes were a requirement."

"That is so," granted the Doctor. "Curiously, I had the opposite impression. I thought the vested choir was the height of form and very aristocratic."

"All wrong," affirmed the Major. "Most democratic scheme for singers ever devised. No form whatsoever. Just a band of plain people, properly garbed, singing the praises of God in the Church. Most reverent too. Nothing so irreverent as finery in the Church. Too distracting. Too self-approving."

"I once sang bass in a chorus choir," said the

Doctor, laughing. "I left when the tenor got a new suit."

"Exactly," said the Major. "Uncomfortable, eh?"

"Just beginning to practice medicine and had too few patients. No new suit for me!"

"Your choir was too aristocratic," was the Major's final comment.

"That opens up the subject of the general sensitiveness of human beings," began the Judge. "They are just as sensitive in their spiritual natures. You like to have your patients in a cheerful room, do you not, Doctor?"

"Surely. Most necessary!" answered the Doctor.

"The Church likewise desires to impress the people with the cheerfulness of religion. But you do administer medicine, Doctor."

"It helps," was the Doctor's comment.

"The Church must administer its truth and healing power, too. It has proper seasons for every phase of its teachings. We use different colors to suggest the general nature of the season. Last Sunday we used white. It is the symbolic color of joy. We use also purple, green and red. Each is suggestive of the particular truths which are being impressed in lesson and sermon. Nature has taught us that art."

"You can't go far wrong in following Nature," said the Doctor.

"Quite right. And human nature too. Those who think the Episcopal Church is artificial are entirely mistaken. It is as natural as Nature herself. The Church through long experience has learned what human nature craves. Beauty, warm associations, pleasant environment, gracious clinging memories, forms of sound words, bright pictures for the mind, suggestions of spiritual mysteries, acts of personal worship, habits of reverence, a consciousness of a great Household in which cluster great ideals, the knowledge of the riches of the past brought to the heart of the present; all these things make the abiding impressions that fill the worshipper with feelings that never depart. The member of the Episcopal Church who feels these things never leaves this household. Religion to him would seem barren, ever after, without the riches and associations of the Church to enforce the lessons and deepen his sense of spiritual things."

"I have heard of one other general impression of your Church which I wish to ask about. Some people think it is like the Roman Catholic. In what respect does it differ?"

"It is difficult, Doctor, to deal with that objection in a word. That impression arises largely from pure prejudice. But the main points of difference are these. We have a different organization. There is no papacy to which we owe allegiance. We differ in doctrine and in worship. We differ in the kinds of spiritual exercise provided for our people, having no compulsory confession. We differ in the intellectual and moral freedom guaranteed to our people.

"It is true that the Roman Church also has historic continuity from Apostolic days, and has an active type of worship, with teaching through the eye. But this latter method, far from being objectionable, is highly desirable, and is not the real ground for the objections of many to the Roman Catholic Church. Do you not know that most lodges and fraternal orders have a ritual and so called 'forms' that far outstrip in their elaborateness the Episcopal Church? Men enjoy these things when they understand them. I never heard a member of a fraternal order call his organization like the Roman Catholic Church, because the officers wore uniforms and the lodge used regalia."

"You certainly have given me something to think about," said the Doctor. "I shall be there next Sunday to try it once more in the light of what you have said."

CHAPTER II.

THE ACTIVE WORSHIP OF THE PEOPLE.

"WELL, I went to church again," said the Doctor, as if challenged, when the four friends had gathered for their weekly conference in the Rector's study.

"Get the habit!" suggested the Major. "Habits are great supports to life. They relieve the mind of a vast amount of strain."

"Some habits do," admitted the Doctor.

"I am speaking of habits of which we approve," replied the Major with a trace of humor in his voice. "The trouble with most people is that they begin every Saturday night to decide whether or not they will go to church Sunday. It is always an open question. They struggle with it on Sunday morning, until the mind is worn out with perplexity. Any chance occurrence comes in to turn the scale. A visitor, a late morning paper, a failure to consult the clock, a flat tire, a dozen little things, determine the decision adversely. Habit would overcome all this."

"You are quite a philosopher, Major," asserted the Doctor.

"Not at all. Only an observer. It is never an open question as to whether or not a man will go to his business on Monday morning, even if he might remain away or be late. His decision about that has been made once for all. Habit does the rest. Nothing is so satisfactory and so beneficial as to let habit carry you on. People torture themselves by indecision. A course of action, firmly established, would relieve them of countless mental confusions.

"So you think church-going can become a habit?" asked the Doctor.

"Nothing easier!" affirmed the Major. "Never let it be an open question, never let a Saturday night's indecision or a Sunday morning's wavering disturb you. Just get up and go."

"That's a good thing," said the Doctor, "if you are certain that you want to go."

"Why shouldn't you want to go?" asked the practical Major.

"That's too big a question to answer in general," replied the Doctor. "I wanted to go last Sunday and I went. I wanted to see the church in the light of our discussion last week."

"We should be glad to hear your conclusions," said the Judge.

"I am hardly ready to pronounce judgment, most learned Judge," parried the Doctor. "I believe that your view of the Church is the result of more experience than is afforded by attendance at two services."

"Quite so!" admitted the Judge. "But that is true of every valuable thing in the mental or spiritual life. The Episcopal Church must not be judged by casual observation and its wealth cannot be appreciated by casual attendance. To appreciate it you must become accustomed to it. But it is worth the time and the effort."

"I found that what you had said modified my point of view and removed certain prejudices against the Church," admitted the Doctor, "but some new difficulties arose as others vanished," and he glanced at the Rector.

"Be perfectly frank," urged the Rector. "If you think that I do not understand that there are difficulties, you are mistaken. Moreover I have learned more from men's difficulties than you can imagine. I wish that you men would get over the notion that you are going to shock a clergyman by your difficulties. You should give him a chance by being frank. If you would realize that the clergyman respects sincere men and respects their difficulties, it would bring them closer together. Men who think that a clergyman is going to brand them as unbelievers, or anything else, because they have honest opinions, or that he will overwhelm them with refined abuse, are sadly unaware of the desire of a clergyman to talk things over. Give us your opinion, Doctor, and let us reason together as friends. This is not a debate in which we must win, but a 'diplomatic conversation' in which we may get a better point of view."

"In that case, here goes," asserted the Doctor. "Last Sunday I was under the impression that your service was too formal. I did not see why you should use the book so much, and why you should rise and kneel so often."

The Rector was silent for a moment. Neither the Judge nor the Major came to his aid. It was an old question but one that all felt to be important.

"Let us take things in their order, and get down to the fundamental principles," began the Rector. "Do you remember the young woman in Arnold Bennett's play who asked a scientist who mentioned specific gravity, 'Now what is specific gravity, *in a word?*'"

Everyone laughed. The Doctor nodded his head.

"It takes more than a word to make clear the principle of worship of the Episcopal Church.

If you are prepared for several words, then I can explain."

"Please proceed," requested the Doctor.

"There are two types of human beings," said the Rector, "the active and the passive types. Every educational effort shows the influence of these two types. There are people who are more edified by lectures which they receive and think over, and there are others who are more benefited by teaching and reciting. The latter method gives a readiness to the habit of expressing and stating what they have learned."

"You can learn more quickly by attempting to teach than in any other way," put in the practical Major.

"These two general tendencies have always had an influence in religion and have determined in one way or another the methods of public worship," continued the Rector. "The extreme of the passive type is the quiet mysticism of the Quakers, and a very good type it is, in this clamorous day.

"The extreme of the active type is the camp meeting, which is not so admirable.

"Various churches emphasize this active type, but most of those with which you are familiar are of the pronounced passive kind. The congregation assembles, and then, relaxing into a

THE ACTIVE WORSHIP OF THE PEOPLE

state of passiveness, listens. It is true that they do sing a hymn or two as a concession to the other instinct, but for the rest of the service they listen, first to a prayer and then to a sermon."

The Major here broke in. "I have a high regard for my brethren of other churches, but when I attend their service I find myself slowly becoming someone else, a sort of unusual self, under a kind of restraint, with an unnatural pressure about my mind and heart. I have felt that way at funerals. It is as if for a moment I had put aside my true self, and were merely engaged in being silently present at a function in which it was highly improper to intrude a thought or action or emotion of my own. I seemed to contribute nothing except an impassive countenance and a hearing ear. I felt like a judge who was taking an impartial survey of the occasion but who gave no evidence of his feelings. It was a relief when they passed the plate. I could *do* something then."

"Weren't you silently joining in the service?" asked the Doctor.

"Yes, but there was afforded no opportunity to assert myself. I felt as if I were forbidden to salute when the flag passed, or to arise when the national air was played. There was nothing to give me a chance to declare my faith, or to express my emotions."

"I hope you made the collection a sufficient opportunity to show the depth of your approval," suggested the Judge with a twinkle in his eye.

"Trust me," said the generous Major. "I never had any sympathy for the man who thought he was exempt from that responsibility. But let the Rector go on."

"The Episcopal Church, while it gives large opportunity for quiet and searching meditation, emphasizes the active type of worship. The Church feels that the people need the opportunity of expressing their repentance, their gratitude, their faith, their praises, their prayers. Nothing drives an idea or emotion inward so effectively as to express it outwardly. A singer understands that and is more affected by a great song than any of the auditors. That, plus a voice, makes great singing. To utter your faith, to give it words, drives it into your soul. To express it is to bring an emotion, a spiritual state, into the light, so that its roots may grow with the energy absorbed from without."

"That's true," asserted the Doctor, "but how does it apply to your service?"

"You need only follow the service to see that it provides for the outward expression of every

THE ACTIVE WORSHIP OF THE PEOPLE

religious emotion of the worshippers. They are not a group of people gathered to hear, an audience, but a group of people gathered to participate, a *congregation*. They, and not the minister, perform the act of worship. He is but the leader, the director. The worship ranges through every need of the soul, and for each need there is some corresponding expression.

"For this reason our people stand during certain parts of the service. Standing is the natural attitude during praise. We sit during instruction and kneel for prayer. To sit during an entire service is to allow the passive side of one's nature to predominate. But worship is an active participation in the expressive acts of the service. The attitude of the body reinforces and stimulates the attitude of the mind. The people participate in the worship. They are not a body of listeners."

"It is like the difference between singing in a great chorus and merely hearing a solo," added the Judge.

"If you were a baseball player, which would you rather do," asked the Major, "play in a game or watch a game?"

The Doctor laughed. "I see the point. I'd rather play in the game."

"Exactly. And I think you will find that you

would rather participate in worship than merely attend it," added the Major.

"Many a church whose worship is of the passive type has felt this need," continued the Rector, "and they have tried to meet it by music of the emotional kind. But their chief admission of the need is the institution of the prayer meeting in which the people find opportunity for expression. That is intended to correct the passive character of public worship."

"But do you mean to say that the benefits of the prayer meeting are found in your worship?"

"The two are not exactly alike, but the desire for self-expression that is provided for by the prayer meeting is met every Sunday by the service of the Episcopal Church."

"But no one prays individually?"

"Oh, yes, indeed. Each one does. The only difference is that each one does it without laying bare his individual experience to the gaze of others. There is the utmost individuality in the public worship and yet the privilege of privacy. This is most desirable, because real spirituality is of such a nature that only very rarely does an open expression of spiritual experience prove of benefit to others. But in the public worship of the Episcopal Church each one may express the needs of his heart. If he comes to get the benefit to the full, he comes conscious of the presence of God and the relation of his own soul to God. He brings his sins, his needs, his hopes, his gratitudes, his supplications, his faith. If he does not he is passing by a vital experience of life. There, in an act of repentance, he pours *his* sins before God, in an act of praise he utters *his* gratitude. So with every phase of it. Each soul lives through a vital experience before God, and has opportunity in the most impressive and exalted way to give expression to his own worship."

"Do you mean that that is what church-going is for?" asked the Doctor, slightly puzzled.

"Precisely. What did you think it was for?"

"Well, I had not stopped to analyze it very much. I had rather thought of the sermon as the chief thing."

"The sermon has its place, to be sure. To the heart prepared by worship the sermon comes to guide, to enlighten, to stimulate. The trouble with too many sermons is that neither the heart nor the mind of the hearer is prepared for them. If the sermon prompts to repentance and to prayer it seems unreal unless the church provides opportunity in public worship for the hearer to give expression to them. I know that you will say that repentance ought to reveal itself in acts and in conduct. True. The sermon and the worship together give the spiritual stimulus to acts and to conduct. Each supplies a necessary element to the religious life, but the sermon must not be confused with the worship."

"Then it isn't enough that people just go to church," said the Doctor. "They ought to be"—here he hesitated for a word—"they ought to be *involved* in it."

"Exactly," affirmed the Major, "that's the word. Many go who are not involved."

"I was tempted last Sunday evening to go to a church which held out as an attraction a whistling quartette. I am afraid I didn't go to worship."

"Such a perversion of worship is not worthy," pronounced the Judge. "It may attract crowds, but it cheapens religion. The practice of religion ought to be simple, intelligible, and even popular, in the best sense of that word, but it does not consist in attracting crowds by a promise of novelty or entertainment."

"But the stranger unfamiliar with your worship has no chance. He does not know what to do," urged the Doctor.

"But he may learn," replied the Rector. "It is not so difficult as you imagine. Every accomplishment is the result of practice. You could not play in an orchestra by merely owning a violin.

THE ACTIVE WORSHIP OF THE PEOPLE

Every art is the result of effort. Worship is a great art. One must become skilled in it. The first step is to know the methods and to become familiar with the Prayer Book. This is quite easy. A very little attention and the instruction which every Church provides will do this.

"The next step is more difficult. It is to grasp what the worship is intended for, and how you may spiritually take part in it. That requires knowledge and experience. But it is supremely worth while.

"When one grasps only the idea that the people read a few pages from a book, then he charges the Church with formalism."

"That's what I did exactly," admitted the Doctor. "It seemed a form."

"That's a very superficial judgment. The Episcopal Church cares nothing for forms as such. That which seems a form is merely a framework which supports the substance of worship. The worship is like a great oratorio, in which each attendant has a part. Each musician, however, in an orchestra has a score with the notes upon it. If he recites the notes as do-re-me it would be formal, tiresome and without interest. But he *plays* them. That gives inspiring music. So the worshipper fills the forms with feeling, aspiration, hopes, prayer, and praise."

"But does not that mean a height of worship to which the ordinary man cannot reach?"

"Not at all. Every man living may share to some extent in the oratorio of worship. He may not always analyze and dissect it, but the substance of it will inspire him. And what you call the forms merely direct, suggest, stimulate, and guide. We have no use for forms as such."

"Then you believe in educating the people in appreciation of the substance of worship?"

"Why not? It is a most vital matter. We send our children to school, then to college, and often to universities, that they may enlarge their mental outlook. Is it not worth while to train the people to use their spiritual powers to the utmost?"

"Will the service of the Church do that?" asked the Doctor.

"No," asserted the Rector, "no more than the text books will educate you. You must co-operate. The service is a means, not an end. It is a method, not a result. But every Sunday and every service is a step in the process. Our text book is the Book of Common Prayer."

"That suggests another difficulty," said the Doctor. "Why do you use the Book of Common Prayer?"

"That brings us to the third principle underlying our practice," replied the Rector. "You remember that the first principle is that the Church makes its appeal to the eye as well as to the ear; the second principle is that the Church is democratic in the best sense of that word, encouraging the active participation of the people in expressive worship. The third principle is that the Church provides for the public worship of the congregation by using the Book of Common Prayer. But it is too late to begin tonight. If you care to come again, I'll try to make it plain."

"I'll be here again," asserted the Doctor, as they left.

CHAPTER III.

THE PRAYER BOOK AND PUBLIC WORSHIP.

The following week the Doctor was the first to arrive at the Rector's study. He found the Rector engaged for a few minutes and he spent the time examining the books upon the shelves. Occasionally he took one from its place and turned over the pages. At last the Rector was ready to talk.

"I have been looking at your books," said the Doctor. "They interest me. Men have given religion a good deal of study, haven't they? I never realized that there were so many books dealing with this subject."

"Religion has been the study of man since man began to think," replied the Rector. "There have been a thousand books written for each one I have on these shelves."

"But to what purpose?" asked the Doctor. "We seem as confused about it as were primitive men."

"That is because you have never taken the

trouble to study the subject. Medicine seems chaos to me, yet I suspect that the science of medicine has made progress and has reached some definite conclusions."

"You may be sure that it has," replied the Doctor, "but we have the experience and practice of the ages to rest upon."

"So have we," parried the Rector. "And we have reached some conclusions that are quite as worth while as yours."

"I thought every church and almost every minister developed his own views," said the Doctor.

"If that were not the statement of a grown man I should call it childish," laughed the Rector. "If religion were merely the sum total of each man's guesses, surmises, and views, it would be of no more importance than the guesses of a child about the moon. The Christian religion is a revelation of God through Christ, verified to us by experience, study and practice."

"Why is it not written down in black and white for the plain man?" demanded the Doctor.

"It is," asserted the Rector. "There, your hand is on the book now."

The Doctor took it from the shelf and read, "The Book of Common Prayer."

"Oh," he exclaimed, "I thought that was a book of services for church."

"It is, but it is more. It is a manual of religion. It contains the fundamentals of the Christian Faith. It is a summary of the teachings of the Bible and an exposition of the doctrines of Christianity. It contains all that a Christian need believe to his soul's health."

"But you use it in Church as a service book."

"We do indeed, and it is the most important religious book in the English language, except the Bible."

The Doctor looked at it again and turned the pages.

"I see that it contains a good many things," was his comment. "But just now I am most interested in the question I proposed last week. Why do you use the Prayer Book in worship?"

At this point the Judge and the Major entered. The Judge had heard the question and with a nod to the Rector, he at once began to take part in the discussion.

"So you are at it again, Doctor. I would like to answer your question by asking another. What is public worship?"

"As I said once before, Judge, before you three entered this open conspiracy to enlighten me, I always thought that public worship was singing a few hymns, listening to a prayer and hearing a sermon."

The Judge was serious. "Would you believe me, Doctor, if I should tell you that that is not public worship in the full historic sense of that term?"

"That's public attendance at the private worship of the minister," put in the Major.

The Rector protested. "Don't put it in that way, Major. It's a fashion of public worship, very modern and quite unlike the worship of the ages. It is not what we feel to be sufficient."

"What is worship then?" demanded the Doctor.

"It is the common worship of the people, with the effort to express five great phases of the religious life," began the Judge. "From the earliest days public worship has developed as a great drama of common experience. It has five elements: repentance, prayer, praise, faith, and instruction. Moreover, it is a participation in the great wealth of spiritual power which our Lord intrusted to His Church."

"But why the Prayer Book?" insisted the Doctor.

"That brings us to our third principle, which is that the Episcopal Church provides for the participation of the people in public worship.

THE EPISCOPAL CHURCH

When people come together to share in a service there must be some mode of common expression. There must be some pre-arranged method for common action. The Prayer Book provides the method by which the whole congregation can share in the experience. Otherwise they could not worship at all. Every public worship has some kind of Prayer Book."

"We never had one in the church in which I sang," asserted the Doctor.

"Not this book, perhaps, but another. Did you not read a Psalm together?"

"Yes," admitted the Doctor.

"Was it not printed somewhere?" asked the Judge.

"In the back of the hymnal."

"That was a Prayer Book of a sort, the beginning of one," affirmed the Judge. "When the people gave expression to worship they used what you call a 'form,' printed in the hymnal."

"They did," said the Doctor.

"So when you sang together, did you not use a printed 'form'? Could you imagine the people singing without the printed words? The Prayer Book bears the same relation to the worship that the hymnal does to the singing.

"Every time the people share in the worship they use some sort of a form or pre-arranged

THE PRAYER BOOK AND PUBLIC WORSHIP

method. The reason we use a Prayer Book is that the people may join in the worship."

"Well, I see that," said the Doctor. "It gives the congregation a chance."

"Exactly," said the Judge. "And it does more. It educates them in forms of sound words. It enlarges their knowledge and stimulates their minds."

"Where did you get this book?" asked the Doctor.

"It is the product of ages of devotion," answered the Rector. "Four-fifths of it are the words of the Bible. The rest of it is from the devotions that by reason of their beauty and their spiritual power have endured throughout the centuries. It was first compiled in the English language in the year 1549. It was adapted to the use of the Church in America in the year 1789."

Here the Rector went to his shelves and took down a book.

"Let me read to you some words of appreciation of the Prayer Book, written by men who are not members of the Episcopal Church."

"This is from a Scotch Presbyterian. 'The Prayer Book is the accumulation of the treasures with which the most diversified experience, the most fervent devotion, and the most exalted genius have enriched the worship of prayer and praise during fifteen hundred years,'"

"Another Presbyterian says, 'We have never doubted that many of the purest flames of devotion that rise from the earth ascend from the Altars of the Episcopal Church.'"

"Here is what John Wesley said, 'I believe that there is no liturgy in the world either in ancient or modern language which breathes more of solid spiritual, rational piety than the Book of Common Prayer.'"

"'Dr. Adam Clark, the most learned commentator among Wesley's followers, says: "It is the greatest effort of the Reformation, next to the translation of the Scriptures into the English language. As a form of devotion it has no equal in any part of the Universal Church of God. It is founded on those doctrines which contain the sum and essence of Christianity, and speaks the language of the sublimest piety, and of the most refined devotional feeling. Next to the Bible it is the book of my understanding and of my heart."'"

"'The following is from the memoirs of the learned Congregationalist, Professor Phelps: "The Liturgy of the Episcopal Church has become very precious to me. The depths of its meaning, it seems to me, nobody can fathom who has not experienced some great sorrow. We have lost much in parting with the prayers of the old Mother Church; and what have we gained in their place? I do not feel in extemporaneous prayer the deep undertone of devotion which rings out from the old Collects of the Church like the sound of ancient bells. I longed for, and prayed for, and worst of all, waited for some sublime and revolutionary change of heart; and what that was, as a fact of a child's experience, I have not the remotest idea. If I had been trained in the Episcopal Church, I should at the time have been confirmed, and entered upon a consciously religious life, and grown up into Christian living of the Episcopal type.""'

"'This is the testimony of another gifted Congregationalist of this country, the Rev. Thomas K. Beecher: "I certify that you rarely hear in any church a prayer spoken in English that is not indebted to the Prayer Book for some of its choicest periods. And further, I doubt whether life has in store for any of you an uplift so high, or downfall so deep, but that you can find company for your soul and fitting words for your lips among the treasures of this Book of Common Prayer."'"

"What you have read is very impressive," said the Doctor. "I shall read the Prayer Book more carefully. But one thing I am not accustomed to. I do not understand why you use written prayers. Are they not too formal and rigid?"

"I presume that one not accustomed to them would think them so," admitted the Rector. "But we have good reasons for using them. In the first place, we must use precomposed prayers if the congregation is to take part in public worship. I have already touched that point."

"I understand that," said the Doctor, "but that does not mean that they are of value in themselves."

"Quite right," conceded the Rector. "Now I do not wish to state that spontaneous prayer is not a valuable practice. It is a noble and sincere method of prayer. But the written prayers have both certain advantages in themselves and also in public worship.

"You are falling into the common error, Doctor, of supposing that there are but two types of prayer, the printed prayer of the Prayer Book and the spoken prayer. This distinction applies merely to the realm of appearance. There are really four types of prayer; the precomposed, written or printed prayer; the precomposed memorized prayer; the formal spoken prayer; and the spontaneous prayer.

"The precomposed printed prayer is found in the Prayer Book.

"The precomposed memorized prayer is frequently used by ministers who appear to be speaking spontaneously. They have memorized their prayers, often using the Prayer Book. Every minister is perfectly at liberty to do this."

"The formal spoken prayer is the sort in which the minister adheres to a certain framework but varies the words. This is the usual type of prayer among those who do not use a Prayer Book. Sunday by Sunday it has much the same formal structure and outline, with a little variety of language. It is the prayer in which set phrases occur with frequency. This is actually the most formal of all types of prayer. And it has the disadvantage of being the prayer of the minister alone, not the prayer of the people.

"The spontaneous prayer is less frequent. In it a man prays under the stress of great emotion, or need. But since spontaneity is a matter of human emotion and not a matter of words, it may as quickly find expression in the treasury of prayer in the Prayer Book as in any self-chosen words."

"The printed prayers are not less sincere, then?" asked the Doctor.

"Not necessarily so," replied the Rector. "Any prayer may be insincere. Sincerity is not in the prayer whether written or spoken, but in the heart of him who utters it. You may be quite as lacking in the spirit of worship in merely listening to a prayer as in reading it. It depends upon an inner condition that is quite apart from the method.

"Some men have the gift of prayer; others have not. There is no greater burden placed upon a minister than to utter before a congregation a prayer that really carries upward the hearts and minds of the people."

"But do the written prayers accomplish that?" asked the Doctor.

"They at least enlist every particle of the spiritual energy of the people," said the Rector. "They make the act of prayer a positive act of the person, rather than a mere act of attention. And more than that, they cover every need, every aspiration, every sorrow, every hope of human life. Every person who attends church comes with his particular burden, his especial need. The prayers range over every phase of spiritual experience. They bring comfort to the sorrowing, hope to the burdened, courage to the tempted, joy to the despondent, and forgiveness to the penitent. Everyone who comes to Church with sincerity finds in the prayers some message to his own soul. The congregation in Church is like a group of voyagers on an ocean liner. Each is going on a different errand, for a different purpose, animated by a different motive. Yet for a time they share the same great pathway of an ocean voyage and mould their varied purposes into one great experience. Our services are like that. For a time all sorts and conditions of men share a great spiritual voyage in our service, in which each finds something which blends with his individual purpose. The prayers are so sublime, so free from any but the highest sanctions, so full of the needs of our common human nature, so complete in their religious expression, that no one need seek help there and not find it.

"Moreover they suggest thoughts and aspirations that search our very hearts. They are universal devotional experience pouring its wealth through every mind and heart. They enlighten and inspire and educate the soul."

"But do not the same prayers every Sunday grow monotonous?"

"Not if they satisfy a hunger, Doctor. Do your meals grow monotonous? Not if you are hungry. Human life day by day, with most of us, consists of repetitions of the same acts. Most of our lives consist in doing things that are usual and customary. They do not grow monotonous if such repetition contributes to a great end, a great duty.

"So the needs of men's souls are much the same week by week. They need much the same spiritual food. They need hope, comfort, courage, faith and the sense of God's presence. Variety in prayer may entertain but it will not edify and support the soul. But as a matter of fact the aspect of these prayers is as varied as the customary and monotonous forms of nature. Flowers and trees, clouds and stars, rivers and mountains, abound in nature, yet nature is not monotonous. So we bring a new man each week to share in the fundamental things of God, and each week the prayers glow with a different light and emphasis. They grow monotonous only to him who fails to bring his heart into tune with them."

"But the minister reads them to the people," objected the Doctor.

"No, indeed," urged the Rector. "He is merely the leader. He offers them to God. He interprets them to the people. That is his real part. He should read so that the force of the prayer makes itself plain. He reinforces with his voice that which they read with their eyes. He offers them to God, not to the congregation."

"Moreover," added the Rector, "the written prayers of the Prayer Book are among the finest creations of literature. As such they must be judged as any other forms of art interpretation are judged. We never tire of the masterpieces. Have you ever heard a play of Shakespeare interpreted by a master?"

"Yes, indeed," said the Doctor.

"Did it detract from the experience when you remembered that the actor was uttering pre-composed forms of words, words written several centuries ago? Would it have added to your satisfaction to have the actor extemporize the words?"

"I am afraid not," conceded the Doctor.

"It would not indeed," said the Rector emphatically. "The masterpieces have a power over the soul that will never die because they have something of worth in them for the race. We would go again and again to see the Sistine Madonna, or Hamlet, or Salisbury Cathedral. We do not exhaust them by one seeing, or one hearing. They are a treasury from which the human spirit exacts riches that never fail. Their form is fixed and will remain fixed, but their spirit and appeal are fresh and vital to every human life. So with the great masterpiece of devotion, the Book of Common Prayer. Countless millions have been saturated with its language, its spirit, its truth, and like a great fountain, which has ever the same form, its flowing waters refresh the human soul and renew the human spirit.

"And that is really what we mean by worship. It is not an exercise, a drill, a rehearsing of words, but a great experience, in which, stimulated by the noblest of written words, the spirit of man comes into intimate communion with God."

"Do all feel that?" asked the Doctor.

"Possibly many do not feel it constantly," admitted the Rector. "But it is the purpose of the Church to lead them to feel it. And at times they feel it very keenly. But week by week the Church keeps this ideal before the people and urges them to those devotions and practices by which they may surely upbuild the consciousness of the presence of God in worship."

"Another question before we go," said the Doctor. "May any one use your Prayer Book?"

"Most certainly. It is the possession of Christianity as much as the Bible is. And one thing more, Doctor. It is a book of the home as well as of the Church. If every home had its Prayer Book and if every person would read it daily, there would be such a revival of personal religion as would astonish our nation. Not only does it provide tables of lessons from the Bible which may be read daily, but it contains the Psalms, the daily reading of which is a most profitable religious exercise. The Gospels and Epistles which are in the Prayer Book are a veritable mine of the treasures of the New Testament. The practice of making daily use of the Prayer Book is one that will enrich the life of any person seeking the truths of God. I commend it to every Christian man."

*

CHAPTER IV.

BAPTISM AND CHURCH MEMBERSHIP.

When the Major entered the Rector's study the following week, he found the latter engaged in writing a letter.

"Busy again?" asked the Major.

"I shall be free in a moment," answered the Rector. But before he had finished the Doctor and the Judge had entered.

"Just sending a note to a bishop in Australia," declared the Rector. "One of my boys is going there and I want him to be cared for in his Church."

"Have you a branch in Australia?" questioned the Doctor.

"I hardly know what you mean by that," rejoined the Rector. "The Episcopal Church exists wherever the English language is spoken. This boy is not merely a member of this parish but he is a member of the whole Church, and is consequently entitled to all its privileges wherever he may be. He has spiritual privileges in the whole Anglican communion."

"Then the household of which the Judge spoke last week is very widespread?" queried the Doctor smiling. "A pretty big family."

"Quite right," responded the Major. "The sun never sets on the Church. It girdles the world with towers and steeples."

"And the boy is part of the whole of it," added the Judge.

The Rector had addressed the letter, and had taken a comfortable chair.

"The boy will find in Australia the spiritual privileges to which he has been accustomed, and administered in a way in which he has been educated. That's one advantage of a household having common family traditions."

"But I do not see why you claim your Church to be a household. One is born into a family. If I am right many people enter the Church who are not born in it. You are using a figure of speech, are you not?"

"It is a figure of speech, but it is most exact," affirmed the Rector. "One is born into the Church."

"I don't quite see the analogy," persisted the Doctor.

"Let me explain," suggested the Rector. "There are two forms of Church organization in our land. You are quite familiar with them.

THE EPISCOPAL CHURCH

One might be called the household organization and the other the lodge organization."

"You are born into one, but you join the other," said the Major.

"Many denominations with which you are familiar have the lodge idea of their individual churches. That is to say the person who wishes to be a member of that church makes a definite decision to join it, and by an act or ceremony of initiation he is taken into it. He is then a member of it."

"Isn't that a good idea?" asked the Doctor.

"It has one serious objection," answered the Rector. "It implies that one must come to advanced years before one may be a member of the church. According to this idea church membership is confined almost entirely to adults. The young children are not in the church. To me it seems a very strange notion that a church should consist of adults and should exclude children. During the years in which the children most need the sense of attachment to the church, when they should feel the sense of a definite relationship, they must not be excluded. When they come to early manhood or womanhood, some churches of the lodge idea submit them to a probation, or a trial. If they are good enough they may be allowed to enter into membership. If they fail to meet the standards, which are usually set by mature minds, they are not admitted."

"Never thought of that before," affirmed the Major. "Exactly like a lodge. Keep you out if they don't want you. Rather exclusive, eh?"

"It seems so," continued the Rector. "Now the Episcopal Church has a very different attitude toward the children. It has the household idea. When a child is born what do the parents say? Do they say 'We are going to consider this child as a child at large, unattached and with no permanent ties. If the child grows up to be good and amenable then we shall admit him to the family.' Do they say that?"

"Rather not!" asserted the Major with some warmth. "They say, 'You are the most important member of this family. You do more to incite the family to care and thoughtfulness than any one else. You are always a majority. When you grow up if you are good we shall rejoice, but if you are not good, we shall somewhat blame ourselves, and if we are human we shall hold you closer to the home. At any rate, good or bad, you are a part of it and no matter how far astray you may go, the father's care and the mother's love will keep your place for you. You will never forfeit your place, your seat in the family circle.' That's what the real family says." And the Major pounded his fist on the arm of the chair.

"That's what the Episcopal Church says too," added the Rector. "The Church admits even babes into membership in the Household of the faith. They become members, not with full privileges as yet, even as children of the family have not the privileges of the adult, but just as much members of the Church as a baby is a member of the family. Why should they not be? Is the Church of the living God a place in which babes and children have no real membership? For my part," and the Rector's eyes blazed with conviction, "I should not care to be a member of a church that would not admit my baby. I want my baby, from its earliest years, when it begins to have knowledge of its relations, to have three convictions: first, that it is of a land where the flag means protection and inspires patriotism; that it belongs to a family which surrounds it with love; and that it belongs to a Church where God and the good, the discipleship of Christ and the idea of service are a very part of the air it breathes."

"Then you mean to say," submitted the Doctor, "that your children are as much members of the Church as yourself?"

"I mean that exactly," affirmed the Rector. "They were born into the Church by baptism. Later they will have the full privileges."

"And they became members of the Church by baptism?" asked the Doctor.

"Yes, by the sacrament of baptism. Our Lord Jesus Christ founded a Kingdom which was to endure upon the earth. He even went so far as to call it His Kingdom, which is another way of saying that it was a real expression and part of Himself. It was not the device of man, or the decrees of church councils, but the very provision of Christ Himself, that baptism was made the means of entrance into that Kingdom. He who is baptized becomes a member of Christ's Kingdom. This is true of every baptized person."

"Does one baptized in your Church likewise become a member of it by baptism?"

"He does. The Episcopal Church is historically a part of the Kingdom of God. Now, Doctor, I do not wish to be misunderstood when I refer to other churches. They are great bodies of Christians, doing untold good, and embracing in their membership many gifted and saintly souls. They indeed arouse our admiration. They have helped to convert the world to Christ. In my reference to them I am simply trying to make clear that they have a different origin, a different structure, and a different method from our own. We admit of them everything which they claim for themselves. They do not claim to be historic churches. The Lutheran Church was founded in comparatively recent times, namely in 1529. The Methodist Church originated in 1766. The Disciples were organized in 1812. No denomination of today was in existence before 1523.

"Nor do they claim a historic ministry. Most of them proclaim a ministry selected and empowered by a congregation. We admit their claims.

"They ought to do no less for the Episcopal Church after an examination of the evidence. We claim and we have, a historic ministry. And we claim and have had historic existence from Apostolic times.

"The Episcopal Church is a historic part of the visible Kingdom of God. It is not the whole of the Kingdom, but a part of it. For you must remember that when our Lord established His Kingdom on earth it had a visible organization, with its ministry and its disciples. That original organization has not ceased to exist; through all the centuries it has persisted. Although it has not kept its original unity, the living parts remain, and the Episcopal Church in America is one of those parts. Our history runs back nineteen centuries. He who by baptism becomes a member of the Kingdom of God, is likewise, if such be the intention of the one who baptizes, a member of the historic expression of the Kingdom which still remains as the evidence of the invisible realm in which God brings men's souls into union with Himself. That act of baptism is an act of union with the visible portion of the Kingdom, His Church, if such be also the intention of the one who performs the baptism. The child becomes a member of the invisible Kingdom and the visible Kingdom by the same act. Consequently, since it is only a matter of plain history that the Episcopal Church is a portion of the original organization and has never lost its historic identity with the Church which Christ founded, it follows that when a priest of the Church performs a baptism he is making the child a member of the Kingdom and of the Church by the same act."

"But the child is too young to know what is being done," objected the Doctor.

"Very true. But the child is not consulted as to the family into which it is born. The parents have assumed that responsibility. They commit the child to many relationships without waiting for it to arrive at an age at which it can be consulted. Its land, its education, its environment are not matters of the child's choice. If the parents believe in God they must certainly feel that they have the duty of bringing the child to God's Kingdom by baptism. Otherwise their convictions about God are not worth mentioning. To deprive the child of a relationship which they value, is to admit that it makes no difference to the child whether or not it becomes a member of Christ, the child of God and an inheritor of the Kingdom of Heaven."

"But when the child grows up, what then?" suggested the Doctor.

"When the child grows up he is given the opportunity to decide for himself whether or not he will accept all the privileges of the Kingdom. That is true even of the family. A grown up boy or girl may accept or reject the family traditions, may accept or reject the high influences and purposes with which a family ought to surround its child. It must make the decision. But the child is still a member of the family. So when a baptized child comes to years of discretion in the Church, the opportunity is given to him to accept for himself the further privileges of the Church, and to enlist himself among those to whom the Church is a real household, full of strength; whose matured judgment, tried purposes, seasoned methods, and age-long sanctions, whose treasures of strength and grace, are of more value to any soul than the self-determined and self-chosen paths, which the individual, unguided, may select. The act by which the child determines to abide by the wisdom and long-tried sanctions of the household of the Church is called Confirmation."

"I always thought Confirmation was joining the Church," said the Doctor.

"Not at all. Confirmation, for one baptized in the Church in infancy, is merely the act by which one comes of age in the Church and is admitted into its full privileges. This is true, however: the Episcopal Church recognizes the fact that any baptism, properly administered, brings the baptized person into the invisible Kingdom of God. The Episcopal Church would recognize your baptism as valid, no matter by what minister you were baptized, if you were baptized with water in the name of the Trinity. But that baptism was not intended to make you also a member of the visible Kingdom, the Church. Consequently your Confirmation in the Episcopal Church, in that case, would be not merely a confirmation of your baptismal obligations, but would be also a recognition of your attachment to a portion of the *visible* Kingdom, the historic

Church, founded by Christ, and existing in this land as the Episcopal Church. A person, so baptized, might be said to have some as yet unclaimed privilege which the Episcopal Church reserves for any baptized person. He may later claim it, and the definite act of claiming that privilege is called Confirmation. That privilege is the right to share in all the spiritual advantages of the historic Church."

"But what if one is baptized as an adult?"

"The principle is the same except that one is then expected to know the obligations to the Kingdom of God involved in baptism. He becomes, just as the child does, a member of the Kingdom, and of the Church, if such is the intention of the service."

"But if an adult is baptized by a minister of the Episcopal Church and thereby becomes a member of the Episcopal Church, why need he take the further step of Confirmation? He has already, in maturity, assumed the baptismal obligation."

"He must be confirmed," answered the Rector, "because Confirmation is more than an individual ratification of the baptismal vows. It is a means by which the gift of the Holy Spirit is bestowed upon each soul, by the imposition of the hands of the bishop. This gift quickens the spiritual life. The baptized person wishes to have this gift. At the same time he wishes to conform to the practice of the ages, and to receive the bishop's blessing."

"If an adult is baptized does the service take place in the presence of the congregation?" asked the Doctor.

"Not necessarily. Most ministers of the Episcopal Church are quite ready to arrange a special service in the church at some hour when the congregation is not present. I have baptized many adults in this way."

"Are there any requirements for the adult who wishes to be baptized?"

"An adult is generally instructed by the minister as to the meaning of the service and of the obligations. At the service itself only four questions are asked to which the replies are given."

The Rector opened a Prayer Book saying, "Here are the questions and answers:

Dost thou renounce the devil and all his works, the vain pomp and glory of the world, with all covetous desires of the same, and the sinful desires of the flesh, so that thou wilt not follow, nor be led by them?

Answer. I renounce them all, and, by God's help, will endeavor not to follow, nor be led by them.

Question. Dost thou believe all the Articles of the Christian Faith, as contained in the Apostles' Creed?

Answer. I do.

Question. Wilt thou be baptized in this Faith?

Answer. That is my desire.

Question. Wilt thou then obediently keep God's holy will and commandments, and walk in the same all the days of thy life?

Answer. I will, by God's help.

"Baptism is naturally followed by Confirmation. The candidate for Confirmation is instructed by the Rector of the parish. The basis for instruction is the Catechism. I would suggest that you read it. It begins on page 266 of the Prayer Book. It is a brief instruction in the Christian faith."

"And what is your Confirmation Service? Must one stand before the congregation and answer questions or make a profession of faith?"

"No. His very presence is an act of professing his faith and no statement is required. The only question put to him is: 'Do ye here, in the presence of God, and of this congregation, renew the solemn promise and vow that ye made, or that was made in your name, at your Baptism; ratifying and confirming the same; and acknowledging yourselves bound to believe and to do all those things which ye then undertook, or your Sponsors then undertook for you?' To which he answers: 'I do!'

"The Confirmation service is the shortest service in the Prayer Book. It is very simple. Those to be confirmed stand before the Bishop. A brief lesson is read, and the question is asked. Then after a prayer, all kneel and the Bishop lays his hands upon the head of each one, saying the Sentence of Confirmation. Then after a prayer the Bishop pronounces the blessing. The service is on page 273 of the Prayer Book."

"Does the confirmed person at once come into the full privileges of the Church?"

"He ought to come at once to his first communion, which is really the great privilege for which confirmation is the preparation. It has been my custom, after confirmation, to instruct the confirmed persons in the meaning, structure, and use of the Service of Holy Communion.

"His life in the Kingdom of God has then reached its maturity, and week by week, he finds in the Service of the Holy Communion the strength, the forgiveness, the nourishment, the guidance, which his soul craves. By it he comes into vital union with God through Christ.

"The Holy Communion thus becomes the chief service of the Church, the height of its worship, and the means by which we realize the real presence of Christ in the life and heart of the worshipper."

"And more than that," concluded the Judge, quietly but impressively, as they arose to depart, "when the solemn words of this service become familiar to the heart and mind, those persuasive appeals and instructions, those loving admonitions and entreaties, those godly injunctions and those comforting assurances, and those sublime statements of the eternal truth and reality of Christ's sacrifice for men, bring a conviction that we speak with truth and appreciation when we refer to our visible and spiritual Kingdom as 'Mother Church.'"

CHAPTER V.

THE APOSTLES' CREED.

The Doctor settled into an easy chair and looked keenly at the Rector.

"You are taking a good deal of trouble to enlighten me," he said at length.

"Why not? Religion is as much a matter for investigation as medicine. It stands the intellectual test."

"Do most people realize that?" asked the Doctor.

"Maybe not. Many people have the religious instinct and seek the place where religion is presented. But I am sure that many desire to know more of the foundations upon which their religious practices rest."

The Judge and the Major entered at that moment and after the usual greetings the four men gathered about the fire.

"Well, Rector," began the Major, "what's the program for tonight?"

The Judge answered. "We are to be enlightened on the subject of the Apostles' Creed."

The Rector looked at the Doctor who nodded assent.

"Let's have sound doctrine," cautioned the Major smiling.

The Doctor was alert in a moment. "Before you begin," he said, "I should like to say that I have always felt that the Church was too much attached to what the Major calls doctrine. The word makes me nervous. Why couldn't the Church have less doctrine and not puzzle us so much?"

The Rector laughed. "What do you mean by doctrine, Doctor?" he inquired.

The Doctor did not answer at once. He was deep in thought. Finally he exclaimed, "I mean abstruse theological statements set forth on authority, but to be believed by the people."

The Rector threw up his hands. "No wonder you want less of it. So do I. You are not defining doctrine. Doctrine is something quite different."

"What is it then?" challenged the Doctor.

"In brief, doctrine is truth, clearly set forth in teachable form. In general, every proposition of geometry is doctrine." Here the Rector reached for a book from the shelf nearby. "This is a book on the Science of Physics. Here is the first law of motion. 'If a body be at rest it will

THE APOSTLES' CREED

remain so unless acted upon by some external force.' That's doctrine."

"But that is a law of science," urged the Doctor.

"Yes, but it is truth set forth in teachable form."

"But the laws of science are different. They can be proved."

"Nevertheless, they are doctrine. Every body of truth, scientific, or historical, or philosophical, or literary, has certain essential principles which men endeavor to express as clearly as possible in order to teach others. Let us get this matter straight in the beginning. Religion has a certain body of truth. When that truth is put in teachable form it is doctrine."

"I heard a man at the club today," said the Doctor, "arguing about the Church. He said that unless the Church abolished its doctrines it would never appeal to him."

"I do not want to slander a possible friend of yours," said the Rector, "but that man was talking sheer nonsense. It sounded big and superior, but it was pure ignorance combined with a little bluster. He wanted to be a liberal fellow, eh?"

"I assumed as much," admitted the Doctor.

"I have no patience with men who think straight on other matters, but who dismiss religion with a phrase that means nothing. No truth has any force until it becomes expressed in doctrine. The multiplication table is pure mathematical doctrine. The rules of Latin grammar are doctrine."

"You are using the word in a general sense," interposed the Doctor. "How about theological doctrine? Is that not more narrow?"

"Not necessarily so," replied the Rector. "There are certain sciences whose truths may not be set forth with mathematical certainty, but which nevertheless may be taught to men. Philosophy is one such science, psychology is another. There are many others. Theology starts with a few fundamental facts. Every known fact is a challenge to investigating minds. Men try to learn the *whole* of the system of which one well established fact is a part. When you have fully established one fact, you are compelled, if you think at all, to draw certain conclusions from it. Robinson Crusoe saw the footprint in the sand. That was a fact. He immediately concluded that a human being had landed on his island. His thoughts revolved about that fact. Take Geology. The discovery of an almost perfect skeleton of a man, in a cave at Mentone, in France, together with the bones of extinct animals, and all covered with stalagmitic crust, is a fact. This together with other facts of a similar nature have set men thinking about the antiquity of man on this earth. Given a fact, thought about it is inevitable."

"Granted," said the Doctor, "but what has that to do with doctrine?"

"Everything," answered the Rector. "Newton saw the apple fall. He noted the fact. His thought about it resulted in his doctrine of gravitation. Now in theology there are certain fundamental facts. Men's thinking about them produces a body of doctrine."

"But what if men draw false conclusions?" objected the Doctor.

"One man is most liable to do so," admitted the Rector. "But the doctrine of the Church is not the conclusion of one man. It is the corporate conclusion of vast numbers of men who have studied, investigated, and verified their conclusions. These conclusions, which the thought and experience of ages have substantiated, are presented as the sound judgment of the Church as to the meaning of the facts."

"But do not doctrines change with the passing ages?"

"Of course. Let us be clear. The facts are eternal and change not. But with the passing of the centuries and with new knowledge, the doctrines change. It is so with every science, your own most of all. The doctrines of the Church represent the highest possible reach of the Church toward the ultimate realities."

"But must people believe them even if they do not understand them?"

"Not at all! Belief in the doctrine of the Church does not mean blind intellectual assent to those doctrines. But it does mean an attitude of confidence in the truth-finding capacity of the Church, and a consequent trust in the conclusions. I have not enough knowledge of medicine to say that I believe, intellectually, in a single one of your prescriptions. Yet I have so much confidence in the whole body of medical science, and in the profession, that I believe in your prescription, if you are not trying upon me some individual experiment of your own."

"But are the doctrines of the Church to be taken like prescriptions?"

"No. The analogy fails there. Good doctrine is quite clear and intelligible. But you cannot swallow it like a pill. Each one can absorb only what he can understand and use. But the Church is a teaching body and it tries to make men understand the doctrine."

"Give an example."

"A fundamental doctrine of Christianity is

THE APOSTLES' CREED

that God is a Person. God is not nature! God is not a mere force, but God is a Person. As such He is capable of love, and He loves men. He wants men to do His will, and He has made clear His will. To those who do His will He promises some supreme experience which we call life eternal."

"Is that doctrine?" asked the Doctor.

"It surely is. Now there are two ways of believing it. One way is to say that it has your intellectual assent as an explanation of God's relation to men. The other way is to admit this statement and this doctrine as a part of your living, as a motive, an incentive and a principle. Then your life shows that you have assented unto it with your whole being."

"You can live doctrine then?" asked the Doctor.

"You cannot do anything else if you really accept it. The Church is only slightly concerned that men agree intellectually that the system of doctrine is reasonable. The Church is tremendously concerned that its teachings become a part of each man's life, and that he base his actions and words upon them."

"Then belief is not merely saying that you think something is true when you do not know whether it is true or not?"

"You must have been under some misguided task masters in your youth, Doctor," broke in the Judge. "What in the world gave you that impression?"

The Major answered for him. "The lack of attention in maturity to the real claims of religion I know. I went through it."

"Belief," said the Rector, "involves the confidence of the whole man in the reliability of the main fact that the world and the race are the products of God's will, and a certainty that those teachings which follow from this fact are trustworthy. Such a belief is the reliance of man upon the validity of human thinking and his faith that the world is not a huge deception arranged for his confusion, but an orderly, reasonable, and loving expression of God's good will and love toward men."

"But does one have to accept the doctrine to become a member of the church?"

"Not in the way you mean," replied the Rector quickly. "The Church's doctrine is the result of the effort of the Church to make clear the implications of the facts upon which it is based. The facts themselves are the important foundations of Christianity. That brings us to the Creed."

"Is the Creed doctrine?"

"In a sense. The Creed is a simple statement of the fundamental facts."

"But I have been told that creeds were hidebound."

"Some misinformed person told you that. As a matter of fact, however, the word creed is very loosely used. Some men use it to describe their individual surmises or opinions. This use of the word is inexact. No one cares a straw about any one person's individual surmises, even if he be a minister. There is a vast amount of nonsense abroad about ministers. There is one opinion that each minister creates his own 'views.' If you like his 'views' you go to hear him. He erects his opinions into a creed. That is as remote from the Christian conception of the ministry of the Episcopal Church, as prophesying about tomorrow's weather from duck's feathers is remote from the work of the meteorological bureau of the United States Government."

"But hasn't any man the same sources of information that you have?" asked the Doctor.

"He seems to have, but he has not used them. A creed is not an individual guess, but a collective assent, verified through centuries, and tested by millions. The purpose of the Church is not to let every man utter his perhaps partial convictions, but to let the whole body speak through its ministry to every hearer."

"I thought each religious body developed its own creed?" suggested the Doctor.

"That brings us to the second error about the use of the word 'creed.' The word is often used to designate man's theories about facts or even one's conclusions about conduct based on those theories. I have heard it said that it is a part of the creed of a certain religious denomination not to dance. That is a misuse of language. The prohibition against dancing is not a part of the creed but is a human provision of discipline. The creed, again, is a statement of the fundamental facts."

"What is the Episcopal creed?" innocently asked the Doctor.

"There is no Episcopal creed any more than there is an Episcopal table of weights and measures. The Episcopal Church did not create a creed. The Episcopal Church is committed to the Apostles' Creed, which is a statement of the fundamental facts of Christianity, and which is so completely identified with Christianity, in the historic sense, that one is inconceivable without the other. The Apostles' Creed is not a series of surmises but a statement of facts. The Episcopal Church teaches those facts to all who seek membership in the Church by the sacrament of baptism."

"And is that all you require?" asked the Doctor.

"With the exception of the expression of one's will to renounce evil and follow God's will, that is all that is asked."

"Do you mean to say that the Church asks you to accept those simple facts, and that it imposes no other obligations whatsoever?"

"Except loyalty to an organization of which you are a part, the Church imposes no other obligation."

"But some denominations exact a promise of their members not to dance, and things of that sort."

"That is the lodge idea creeping out. The Episcopal Church asks only a simple assent to the Creed."

"Do you mean to say that it does not ask you to believe in its method of worship, in the use of the Prayer Book and vestments and such things?"

"I mean that exactly. The Church does not elevate these things into a creed. It thinks that they are valuable as methods. It approves of them. It finds them serviceable. But they are not fundamentally essential. The Church is concerned that you accept God as your Father and Jesus Christ as your Saviour."

"I was under the impression that a church member was under obligation to believe the Bible," urged the Doctor.

"Do not misunderstand my reply, Doctor. The Episcopal Church is the Bible Church. It reads large portions of the Bible to the people in the services; more, I believe, than is read in other kinds of public worship. Every minister of the Church makes solemn affirmation at his ordination that he believes 'the Holy Scriptures of the Old and New Testaments to be the Word of God, and to contain all things necessary to Salvation.'

"But the Church imposes no such obligation upon its members. The Bible is a very large book. The meaning is often obscure. Isolated passages may be found with which to prove almost anything under the sun, if the Bible is accepted as a collection of isolated texts each one of which is considered to be true, irrespective of the rest and unrelated to the context.

"Nor is it a book of science. The statement of Genesis that the world was created in six days is not a literal fact, if we mean six days of twenty-four hours. The Bible cannot be quoted in defense of such a conclusion. The Bible sets forth spiritual and religious truth and in every sphere it reflects only the condition of knowledge which prevailed at the time at which the books were written.

"The Bible is the literature of a great race, the literature of a great movement toward realizing the relation of God to men. As such it is a vast treasury of light and spiritual power, and men may indeed find in it all things necessary to salvation.

"But the Church does not ask you to make a formal statement of belief in the Bible. The Church will instruct you in its truths, but it requires of you no statement of your attitude toward the Bible. The Church believes that as years pass you will learn the truths of the Bible and their appeal to your life will awaken your response to their enduring value to your soul.

"Moreover the Church believes that it has presented the heart of the Bible's *requirements* in the two sacraments of the religious life, Baptism and the Holy Communion, and in the summary of facts, essential to Christianity, in the Apostles' Creed."

"Read me the Apostles' Creed," said the Doctor.

The Rector took a Prayer Book and read the Creed:

"I believe in God the Father Almighty, Maker of heaven and earth:

"And in Jesus Christ his only Son our Lord: Who was conceived by the Holy Ghost, Born of the Virgin Mary: Suffered under Pontius Pilate, Was crucified, dead, and buried: He descended into Hell; The third day he rose again from the dead: He ascended into heaven, And sitteth on the right hand of God the Father Almighty: From thence he shall come to judge the quick and the dead.

"I believe in the Holy Ghost: The Holy Catholic Church; The Communion of Saints: The Forgiveness of Sins: The Resurrection of the body: And the Life everlasting. Amen."

"I am not sure that I understand all that it means," said the Doctor.

"Possibly not at the first reading," agreed the Rector, "for there are several phrases here whose meaning is not quite apparent. A little patient study, however, will make them plain. I always explain these phrases to those who enter my confirmation classes.

"You must understand, Doctor," continued the Rector, "that this Creed is centuries old. It is the collective judgment of the Christian Church as to the fundamental facts. It is as much a corporate expression of the whole Church as it is a personal expression. An individual might not understand all the bearings of these facts. He would scarcely be expected to believe the Creed as the independent conclusion of his own thinking. He might never have discovered some of these facts by himself. The heart of the Creed is this. First, that God is the Father: that Jesus Christ is His Son and was born into this world and died for men; and that the Holy Spirit of God is now active and present to bring men into relation with God. If all that you feel about God and Christ is *toward* these conclusions, then you may, with real integrity, say you believe the facts of the Apostles' Creed. No man can do more than believe *toward* this great expression of fundamental Christianity."

"But it does not explain anything," urged the Doctor.

"It does not. But it is an expression of allegiance toward God and Christ. The teaching Church instructs the attentive mind. But this teaching, as I said, imposes no obligation except as all truth demands credence by its very nature. What I mean is that in the Episcopal Church you do not commit yourself beforehand to a body of doctrine which prevents your own thinking. The Creed does not restrain your liberty of thought, but enlarges it by giving you some basis of fact upon which thought may exercise itself. You have complete intellectual freedom in the Church.

"For, you see, the Creed is an expression of one's sense of security in God's government of the world and in His love for men in the life and death of Jesus Christ. It is an affirmation of the conviction of one's soul that Jesus Christ is the Son of God and the Saviour of men. It is not merely a series of disconnected sentences, having no relation to one another, but it is an expression, in language as simple as can be, and comprehensive of every important fact, of the great central truth. If one of these statements is true, all are true. They unfold, one from another. Anyone who admits the rational character and logical cogency of one theorem of geometry, has necessarily given his assent to the whole system of geometry, even though some of the problems may puzzle him. So, any one of the facts of the creed, standing without the others, is indefinite and obscure. They are an interlocked statement of the whole group of truths. If you can say, 'I believe in God the Father Almighty,' you can say the rest, for the same validity which pertains to this statement, pertains to all. The understanding of this relation is a matter of study. After all, the Creed is a symbol of one's conviction that God has loved men, and that with His love has come a definite effort to illumine and save men.

"And then you must remember, Doctor, that no man has ever reached the final implications of any one fact. The good old sun has warmed this earth for centuries. I believe in that sun. I know his power, his warmth, his cheer. But astronomers today are more diligent than ever in studying the sun. I am mildly interested in their speculations, but I believe strongly in the sun. He is the source of physical energy on earth and I know it. Practically the sun is indispensable to our living.

"So the religious life, after all, is not a matter of trying to reach the bottom of things to satisfy one's intellectual curiosity. It is an intensely practical matter. So, as a matter of fact, I know that they who serve God grow in blessedness and peace and usefulness; those who accept Christ have not only a guide but a motive power, a real inward treasure of thought, of hope, of content. For them there is light ahead and a path, and their minds dwell richly on things eternal. The Church has always been the environment in which this belief and faith in God and Christ have been emphasized, enforced and nurtured. The history of the Church has been a history of care for human souls, human lives. Those who have whole-heartedly entered its portals, have been refreshed, inspired, and given a new heart and a mind richly furnished with true wealth. And the mind of the Church has thought upon the origin of its strength, while the heart of the Church has applied it and the hands of the Church have fought to keep the race clean. The mind of the Church has found in the Creed the sufficient statement of the facts, which, translated into heart power, have so completely enveloped human lives with a sense of the nearness of God and union with Christ. With my whole heart I can say these words which the Church has erected as the intellectual basis of a faith that has wrought miracles among men in transforming the race into the children of God."

"That's the real test," admitted the Doctor. " 'By their fruits ye shall know them.' "

"Wherever those facts have been the basis of corporate action; wherever they have entered men's hearts as the fundamental things of God, the people have been strengthened and religion has had power. But wherever men have thought it possible to erect some less enduring structure, where they have substituted their surmises for this great body of truth, their religion has grown thin and pale, and has finally lost its hold upon the mind and heart of men. Faithful adherence to the Creed has been the strength of the Church throughout the centuries."

The Judge arose. "I have said the Creed all my life," he said solemnly. "I hope that I may say it with firmer conviction on the day of my death. For life would be poor indeed if my dying lips could not fervently say, 'I believe in the forgiveness of sins, the resurrection of the body and the life everlasting.'"

*

CHAPTER VI.

THE HOLY COMMUNION.

When the Doctor entered the Rector's study the following week he found the Judge already there and in earnest consultation with the Rector.

"Planning a new drive?" he asked.

"We are," answered the Judge. "We are arranging for the services this summer."

"Don't you close the church in summer?"

"No, indeed. Services as usual all summer. Why make an exception of summer?"

"Well, there seems to be no particular reason, I admit, except that the people generally take a vacation."

"Possibly so. But Sunday is Sunday even in summer, and to close the Church is to ignore that fact."

"The fourth commandment holds good in warm weather," said the Doctor smiling.

"See here, Doctor," exclaimed the Judge. "You carry about a peculiarly large stock of erroneous notions. Do you think that we observe Sunday because of the fourth commandment?"

"Don't you?" parried the Doctor. "I never gave the matter much thought."

"Gather 'round the fire," commanded the Judge. "Rector, what about Sunday?"

"There is a false notion in many quarters that we are living in Judea, in the year 1000 B. C., instead of in America in the twentieth century. The commandment to keep the seventh day holy applied to the pre-Christian period. The Christian Sunday has an entirely different origin."

"Go on, Rector," urged the Doctor. "This is real news."

"News that is centuries old," continued the Rector. "The early disciples came together on the first day of the week, to observe it as the day on which our Lord rose from the dead. Sunday is not the Jewish Sabbath. Each Sunday is an echo of Easter. Each Sunday is a festival, a day of joy."

"It wasn't so in my youth," commented the Doctor. "It was a day of sadness and gloom. It was oppressive and irksome."

"You were not keeping a Christian Sunday then, but some echo of the early Jewish Sabbath, with a large infusion of puritan piety."

"It was anything but joyous," said the Doctor.

"Sunday is a great day of rejoicing, when properly understood. It is a miniature Easter."

"Did the early disciples so keep it?" asked the Doctor.

"They did. They met on Sunday to celebrate the Holy Communion, the great feast of praise and thanksgiving, the Holy Eucharist. For long over a thousand years this was the chief service of Sunday. The public services to which many of the people of this land are accustomed, that is, a few hymns, a long prayer and a sermon, are very modern."

The Major had entered and was listening.

"They lack imagination, variety, and, often, the suggestion of joy," he stated.

"The Holy Communion has every essential of individual and corporate worship blended in one great spiritual act," continued the Rector. "It is the chief service of Sunday."

"I didn't know that," said the Doctor. "How often do you have this service?"

"In most Episcopal Churches the Holy Communion is celebrated every Sunday. Often it is at an early hour. But this service and the observance of Sunday are so closely interwoven that to let a Sunday pass without this sacrament is to rob Sunday of much of its significance.

"I should like to understand a little more about it," declared the Doctor. "I never understood quite what you meant by a sacrament."

"Speaking in theological terms, a sacrament is an outward and visible sign of an inward and spiritual grace. But we may understand this better if we realize that the word sacrament might have the general sense of an outward and visible sign or token of some inward value. For example," and the Rector took a bill from his pocket, "here is a piece of paper. It is printed and stamped under authority. If I give it to you it conveys one dollar's value. It is a sacrament, speaking generally."

"All life," he continued, " has constant sacramental expression. I wish, for example, to send a message to you. That message has its first existence in my own mind. I write it upon paper. That paper and those ink marks are sacramental. They convey the message. When you read it, the message becomes a reality of *your* mind. The paper and ink may convey anger, joy, sorrow, or whatever I feel. They may produce feelings in you. They are the channels of value.

"Here is a book. It is so much paper, pasteboard, cloth, and ink. Yet it brings from one mind a value to thousands of minds. It is sacramental, an outward and visible sign of inward value. A book may make you cry or laugh. Really it is the author who does so. The book is the effective means of conveying truth from the mind of the author to the reader.

"So with our food. A few acres of land will sustain a man's life. How? Does he eat the earth? No! But he prepares it and plants wheat. He gathers the wheat, grinds it into flour, bakes bread and eats the bread. The loaf has gathered up the chemical elements in the earth and air and sunlight, and conveys them to man to sustain his life. The loaf is a sacrament: it is the outward token of invisible values.

"God's grace toward man, His love toward man, are universal. But He has established certain ways by which men may be assured of God's favor. Jesus Christ ordained the Sacrament of Baptism by which men are incorporated into His Kingdom.

"Jesus Christ died for men. That men might receive the value of His life and death, He instituted the Sacrament of the Holy Communion.

"The consecrated bread and wine are made the very sacraments of the value created for men by the death of Christ on the Cross, and they are the very means by which the power and efficacy of His body broken and His blood shed are conveyed to each individual soul.

"Of course, he who receives them must receive them with a heart prepared to accept them for what they are. There is no magic in them. The individual must be prepared to welcome Christ, His power and love, into the life. The Bread and Wine then become the food of the soul, by which we become partakers of Christ's most blessed Body and Blood.

"Then the sacrament, instead of being an unusual and exceptional method," said the Doctor, "is merely the most natural method, having a counterpart in every process by which life is upbuilt."

"That is quite true," answered the Rector. "The exceptional element is not the method, that is, the charging of bread and wine with some further function, but the exceptional thing is the nature of the value that is conveyed by them. Christ instituted this method and pledged His word that in the Holy Communion there should be the value created by His death on the Cross for men."

"Doesn't nature, which is another manifestation of God, work in a similar fashion in the healing of the ills of the body?" questioned the Major earnestly.

"What do you mean exactly, Major?" asked the Doctor.

"Who heals disease, you or nature?" asked the Major directly.

"Not I," admitted the Doctor. "Nature is the great healer. I simply adjust nature to the purpose."

"Exactly. Now for a certain kind of ailment, nature provides a certain remedy. Is not that remedy, that medicinal force, confined to certain substances?"

"It is," said the Doctor.

"Yet it is nature that functions through that outward and visible substance," said the Major. "It is nature's way. She acts through sacraments. And nature is merely a manifestation of God."

"I see what you mean, Major," granted the Doctor. "But what are the exact benefits which one receives in the Holy Communion?"

"Before I answer that, let me suggest one consideration. Is it not true, Doctor, that the attitude of the patient toward the healing power, whether toward the physician or his medicine, is a large element in the effectiveness of his treatment?"

"You mean confidence in the recovery through the treatment? Yes. It is perhaps the most important element."

"So with the Holy Communion. I suggest that you take your Prayer Book and study the service from the standpoint of the education of the one who receives the Holy Communion; of the way in which the Church endeavors to arouse the consciousness of the need and at the same time inspires a confidence that the need will be met.

"You will find that the Church leads the worshipper through two phases of the great drama of human life. On the one hand the Church, in this service, goes to the very heart of sinful human nature and tries to awaken the soul of man to the deadliness of sin. The Church presents the dignity and worth and satisfaction of human life and the joy of it when sin is overcome and life is filled with the spirit of God. At the same time the Church presents the other phase of the drama, the effort of God to bridge the gulf between man and God created by sin, and to reach forth to bring men to Himself, to reconcile them to Him. Then there is presented that which is the very basis of Christianity, the sacrifice of Jesus Christ, His death on the Cross, that effected the full, perfect and sufficient satisfaction to God for the sins of the whole world. The worshipper cannot be unmoved by the tender mercy of God toward himself. The worship, if it has been effective, brings to man a realization of his supreme need of God. This realization bares many things to himself. It makes him see that sin has in some way entered his life, that he is worldly, or selfish, or worse. It makes him realize his ingratitude in accepting the gift of life and then allowing it to serve merely temporal ends that perish. It lets him see that at death he will be a bankrupt. It produces a hunger and thirst after righteousness. It produces a desire to be a spiritual person, thinking great, true thoughts, doing great, kind deeds, devoting his capacity to the upbuilding and not the uprooting of every righteous effort upon earth. This great drama is a great awakening. Then comes the climax of it all. It is the very effort of God to reach that soul and refresh and strengthen it. So the communicant comes to the Altar, and in a most solemn way and with receptive heart, receives the consecrated Bread and Wine, through which and in which, the power and efficacy of Christ's sacrifice for him are brought to his soul. It is a near approach to Christ that men experience, when with true penitent heart and lively faith they receive these holy mysteries, as pledges of God's love."

"But must not men be very holy in their lives to receive the Holy Communion?" asked the Doctor.

"The Church itself has set forth the conditions under which one is urged to come to the Holy Communion. Christ instituted this sacrament to draw men to Himself, not to frighten them away. No man need question his fitness, only his motive and intention and purpose. Here are the words of invitation:

"Ye who do truly and earnestly repent you of your sins, and are in love and charity with your neighbors, and intend to lead a new life, following the commandments of God, and walking from henceforth in His holy ways; Draw near with faith, and take this holy Sacrament to your comfort.

"If such is your purpose then you may come without hesitation. You must remember that the value of the Holy Communion to any man, is to be determined by experience, not by any process of reasoning unaccompanied by experience. Many a person has found in spiritual exercises, such as prayer and participation in the Holy Communion, great spiritual power, and strength to resist temptation, which he could never find were he content to do no more than reason about them. One of our Lord's most urgent injunctions is to do His will, and knowledge of the power of His injunctions will follow. *Trust* and *act*, has been the watchword of many a powerful life.

"Life is always a struggle," continued the Rector. "If one willingly and gladly surrenders to evil and is satisfied, he should not dare to come to the Holy Communion. But if one fights and struggles, if one wills to overcome evil and wills to free himself from its power, then he may come. It is not a sign of righteousness attained, but of righteousness desired. It is to help men, not to crown saints. It is for sinners, but for sinners who would not willingly remain so. It is a refreshment for the battle, not a reward for the victory. So honest men, however far short they may be of their ideals, may come honestly, if they want God's help."

"Does every communicant realize this?" asked the Doctor.

"Maybe not at first," admitted the Rector. "Spiritual things are not discerned by the eye of flesh. Not every man realizes the value of friendships. He debases a friendship by making it serve some personal end, then loses it and only too late realizes that what he hoped to gain selfishly was of no value compared with the satisfaction in the friendship which he sacrificed. Not every man perceives that his work is a blessing, an opportunity to create, to grow, to have some definite usefulness which men respect, to give some outlet to his powers, to occupy and engage his attention, to give some means of expression to his personality. He may look upon it as mere work, a way to earn a living. He aims to become superior to the necessity of work, and when free from the opportunity to work, he begins to shrink and shrivel. He is an unattached and unrelated energy, turned to self destruction. He becomes unhappy and finally despairs. Life has no joy for him.

"Not every man perceives his relation to God. He does not realize that peace, love, joy, long suffering, gentleness, and goodness are the very things which he had hoped to gain when he was directly aiming at power and possession. He does not realize that serving God brings at once the things which he hoped to find at the end of a long hard task.

"Not every man is sensitive to beauty or joy. It requires greatest self-control, a sublime sense of proportion, a keen sense of values, and a robust faith in the present, to extract the immediate wholesome values of the passing hour.

"So not every man is conscious of his greatest need, the need of spiritual power. When he first comes to the Holy Communion he may do so for reasons which are not the reasons of the one who has learned to see God. But later, when the sense of the passing of temporal things seizes him, when sin assails, or sorrow sears his heart, when his own human strength gives way, and he sees life in its larger relations, when his petty successes which once gave him such complete self reliance and independence, and made him so confident in his ability to face life alone, when such successes fail to avert the tragedies of our daily experience, and the man feels the human foundations tottering, then he will come to his communion with a more complete conformity to God's will, with more earnest desire to make God a partner in life's enterprises. Then he will see the truth of the saying that 'the things that are seen are temporal, but the things that are not seen are eternal.'"

"The Episcopal Church, I assume then, believes in the growth of the spiritual life," said the Doctor.

"Precisely. The Episcopal Church sets forth, in this service, in words of supreme beauty and power, the truth of the development of spiritual capacity and achievement. Slowly but surely its children are educated. Righteousness is no chance product, no hot-house flower dependent upon the emotional appeal of some revivalist, but the steadily rising structure of a Christian life. Every moral law, every spiritual substance, every righteous principle, every reasonable faith, every certain hope, every precept of Christ, every virtue and every beauty of holiness is builded into the growing character. That is the ideal. And the crowning practice and supreme spiritual achievement and active expression of strength, the complete appreciation of the spiritual forces and truths, all find expression in the devout life of the communicant, in the weekly celebration of the Holy Communion.

"It may take years to come to the full understanding of it all, and to find in this service a spiritual exercise and refreshment of the most sublime and exalted character, but this realization finally crowns faithfulness.

"So the Episcopal Church has ever fresh treasures for its people. They do not exhaust its wealth at a bound. Year after year the Church opens up new vistas of truth, new strengths to be attained, new avenues of effort, new reservoirs of power.

"The child at the Altar is giving expression to the simple melody of trust in Christ and obedience to the simple rules of life and conduct which he may understand. But the man at the Altar is giving expression to the great oratorio of worship, with its minor chords which experience has woven into his life drama, with its complex themes such as life has written for him, with the crash of tumultuous notes that work and burdens and defeats have created, but it closes with the climax of harmony which reveals the surrender of his individual will to the will of Almighty God.

"So the man at the Altar is the conqueror, master of himself, bending wayward human impulses to God's plan, strong in his convictions, tender in his judgments, certain in his faith, fervent in his good works, and confident in Christ his Lord and Saviour."

The Rector ceased, and rising, walked to his desk. Resting his head on his hands he added, somewhat wearily,

"I would to God that my people might realize the richness of life which the Church is holding forth to them. They would never fail in faithfulness could they see the unsearchable riches of Christ, instead of always gazing upon the earthly vessel which contains them."

CHAPTER VII.

THE HISTORIC MINISTRY.

WHEN the four friends gathered together the next week the Doctor brought an accusation against the Rector.

"You were not at home last Sunday. I went to church and you were not there."

"No. One has to get away once in a while. I was attending a service of ordination in the Cathedral."

"You mean that some one was made a minister there?"

"Yes, and more than that. A young deacon was ordained priest."

"Do you have priests in the Episcopal Church?" asked the Doctor.

"Of course. I am a priest." answered the Rector. "Why not?" he challenged.

"Well, I have been accustomed to the titles minister, or preacher, or parson, but not the title priest."

"It is a perfectly good word, Doctor. You are not one of those men, I know, who object to using a good word in its proper sense, merely because the popular mind has given some restricted meaning to the word."

"No, I think I would use a word in its proper sense," said the Doctor thoughtfully. "I imagine it is a matter of bringing up. I have associated the word with the Roman Church."

"That is quite correct," answered the Rector. "But it is simple ignorance, to speak plainly, to restrict the use of the word to the Roman Church. There are thousands of priests not of the Roman Church."

"Well, I see I am in for another exposition," said the Doctor laughing.

"Queer study, this matter of titles," interjected the Major. "Never did quite understand why men of your profession were called ministers, clergymen, preachers, rectors and priests. Do they mean the same thing?"

"Not at all, Major," answered the Rector. "They refer to different activities and functions. A man may be any one of them, or perhaps all of them, but they are not the same."

"Elucidate," prompted the Major briefly.

"The broadest term is minister. A person who ministers to another is properly a minister. A nurse is a minister; doctors are ministers."

"News to me," affirmed the Doctor.

"In a general sense, I mean. When one becomes a minister of religion he becomes a clergyman. The word clergyman, however, is commonly used only of ministers of the Episcopal Church.

"If the minister preaches, he becomes a preacher. To use the word preacher to designate a minister is a most awkward and indiscriminate way of speaking. It has arisen from the fact that in many of the public services of which I spoke some time ago, the preaching has been the prominent part. A man stopped me on the street the other day and asked 'Are you a preacher?' I answered 'Frequently,' and that seemed to confuse him. It is literally true. I am a preacher about twice a week.

"A rector is a priest in charge of a parish. The word means ruler. It refers to his responsibility as the chief executive of a parish. A man may be a priest without being a rector. I know several priests who are teachers."

"That is clear," said the Doctor, "but what is a priest?"

"A priest is one who has been ordained by a bishop to the priesthood. A priest may also become a preacher, a teacher, or a rector of a parish. It is an order of ministry to which he is duly set apart, and which he cannot relinquish except by being deposed. The priest of the Church not only is a minister, in that he serves the people, not only a parson, in that he serves as a clergyman, not only a preacher, but he is the authorized officer of the historic Church, to baptize, to administer the sacraments, and to make the authorized statement that God forgives the sins of the people."

"Cannot any minister do all these things?" asked the Doctor.

"He may do many of them, as a minister of Christ, but the priest of the Episcopal Church has authority to do all of them as a representative also of the historic Church," said the Rector plainly.

"Where did the priest of the Episcopal Church get his authority?" asked the Doctor.

"Let me ask you a question, Doctor," put in the Major. "Where did you get your authority to practice medicine?"

"The State gave me a license. I had to study for it," and the Doctor laid emphasis upon his words.

"You could not practice medicine in this State, no matter how hard you studied, if you did not have a license."

"No indeed. Jail," said the Doctor briefly.

"Judge, where did you get your authority to sit on the bench?" asked the Major.

"President's appointment and signed commission," answered the Judge.

"Why cannot our brilliant local lawyer set up a court, Doctor?" continued the Major. "He knows enough law."

"No commission, no authority. I see your point. Go ahead," turning to the Rector.

"Where did you suppose ministers to be created, Doctor?" pursued the Rector.

"I thought that young men studied in theological schools and upon graduation took churches."

"As young men study law and upon graduation begin to practice? You miss one step in the process, Doctor. Your law student must be licensed by the State and become an officer of the court. A young man might be the most diligent theological student in the United States and the most brilliant preacher, but that would not give him *authority*. When he preached he would represent no one but himself. He does not need any special commission to become a preacher and he may connect himself with any religious body he desires, if he conforms to their requirements. But if he becomes a priest of the Episcopal Church he must not only study to pass intellectual examinations, but he must conform to the worship, doctrine and discipline of the Episcopal Church, and then he is ordained to the priesthood by the Bishop. *That ordination gives him authority to exercise his priesthood.*"

"But cannot officers in other churches give authority?"

"They can give such authority as they possess. You must remember that there are two general types of churches, the historic and the non-historic."

"More news," commented the Doctor. "Explain."

"The historic churches are those that can trace their existence and ministry back to the Apostolic Church founded by Christ. These Churches have bishops. The non-historic churches are religious bodies organized by men in recent times. They are like religious lodges. They have no bishops, but various kinds of officers which were arranged for when they were organized. The officers of these non-historic churches may authorize a man to be one of their ministers. That is quite obvious. His authority is solely that of an officer in his own group. The non-historic churches are voluntary associations for promoting religion. But the Episcopal Church is an historic church. It traces its history and ministry to the Apostolic Church, founded by Jesus Christ. He gave authority to the Church and consequently to its ministry. That authority the Church has never lost. By it the bishop ordains men to the priesthood. For example, I am a priest. My authority to minister and rule in religious things is conferred by the bishop who acts for the Church, conferring the authority which Christ committed to the Church. Back of the bishop is the whole body of the historic Church for nearly nineteen hundred years, in which the authority conferred by Jesus Christ has been preserved."

"Do you mean to say, Rector," asked the Doctor, "that your bishops have direct authority from Jesus Christ?"

"I mean that precisely," answered the Rector. "You must remember that Jesus Christ founded an organization, which He called His Church. He was not merely a great teacher, or a great example, but He definitely gave to the human race an organization, which should be the authorized and empowered agent for bringing the world to Him. For this organization, His Church, He set apart certain men, called Apostles, and trained them. He instructed them in their duties, and established the means by which men could be incorporated into that organization, namely, Baptism, and by which they could continue to live in it, namely, the Holy Communion. It was a definite society, and its officers were commissioned in a definite way."

"Where do you learn all this?" asked the Doctor.

"The early records of this organization are called the New Testament. You have heard of that?" asked the Rector smiling.

"Many times," answered the Doctor.

"It is quite plain in that book," continued the Rector. "The first officers of that organization were called Apostles. They enlarged their members and appointed and consecrated successors who should do their work when they themselves died. Those whom they appointed were called bishops. The bishops received their authority and power directly from the Apostles. The bishops consecrated not only their successors, but many other bishops, who enlarged the organization and carried it to many lands. This process has continued throughout all the centuries. Every bishop of the Episcopal Church in the United States has been consecrated by at least three bishops. These in turn were consecrated by earlier bishops. This succession of men, transmitting power and authority can be traced to Apostolic days as easily as the succession of presidents can be traced to George Washington. Do you know why we use the adjective 'Episcopal' in the title of our Church?" asked the Rector abruptly.

"Never thought about it," admitted the Doctor.

"Episcopal is an adjective, from a Greek word 'Episkopos' which is the same word as our Anglo-Saxon word bishop. 'Episcopal Church' means a 'Church having bishops.' The bishops have been the chief pastors and administrative officers in the Church since the beginning. The succession of bishops from the Apostles' day, has never been lost to the Church."

"Do you mean that your bishop who was here last winter, is one of a line of men which has had definite and continuous existence since the days of Christ?"

"I mean exactly that, Doctor. You have stated it precisely. If our Lord had given St. John a ring, and had instructed him to give it to the bishop who was his successor, with directions that the ring was to be handed down to succeeding bishops, that ring might conceivably be in the possession of our own bishop today."

"Of course this line of bishops in America, in direct succession from the English line, is of recent origin," said the Judge.

"To be sure, Judge, Dr. Samuel Seabury was consecrated Bishop of Connecticut by three Bishops of the Scottish Episcopal Church in Aberdeen, Scotland, November 14, 1784. Dr. William White was consecrated Bishop of Pennsylvania and Dr. Samuel Provoost, Bishop of New York, in the Chapel of Lambeth Palace, London, in 1787. These three bishops in America were authorized to consecrate others and in that way the Episcopal Church in America has its bishops. The line of succession extends thus through the Church of England back to Apostolic days.

"From the earliest days the bishops consecrated priests. The word priest is derived from the Greek word 'presbuteros' which means an older man. The priests worked in parishes under the direction of the bishops. A third office of the ministry, called deacon, was also instituted. You may read about it in the sixth chapter of the Acts of the Apostles. A candidate for the priesthood must pass one year in the office of a deacon."

"How many bishops are there in the Episcopal Church in the United States today?" asked the Doctor.

"There are about one hundred and thirty bishops today. Every inch of territory of the

THE HISTORIC MINISTRY

United States and all her possessions is under the jurisdiction of a bishop."

"You spoke of the first three bishops in America receiving their consecration in England and Scotland. What is the relation of the Episcopal Church in the United States to the Church of England?"

"The Episcopal Church in the United States is absolutely independent of the Church of England. Historically we derive our existence from the Church of England, and until the Revolutionary war all Episcopalians in America were members of the Church of England. Our colonies were colonies of England. But when the colonies became independent the Church became independent also. We are in full communion with the Church of England. That means that members of the Episcopal Church in America may go to any church in England or England's imperial possessions and have full spiritual privileges in the parishes. So any member of the Church of England has full spiritual privileges in our parishes. But so far as government is concerned we are absolutely independent. We are not the English Church. We are the American Church."

"Our Church," said the Judge, "is essentially American in spirit and substance. Remember the great Americans who have been members of the Episcopal Church. George Washington was a devout communicant of the Church, and was a vestryman of Truro parish, Virginia, and a member of Christ Church, Alexandria, in which his pew may be seen today.

"Benjamin Franklin was a member of the Episcopal Church. Thomas Jefferson was a member of the Episcopal Church. Two-thirds of the framers of the Constitution were members of the Episcopal Church. It is most impressive testimony to the influence of the Church in colonial days, and also to the staunch Americanism of many of its most conspicuous members.

"The fact is," continued the Judge, "that the general organization of the Church in this land reflects the method of the federal administration because the same minds were directing both organizations. I have often attended the General Convention of our Church, which meets every three years. There are two Houses; the House of Bishops and the House of Deputies.

"The House of Deputies consists of delegates from every Diocese, both clergymen and laymen.

"The whole arrangement is similar to our Congress, with its Senate and House of Representatives.

"This Convention meets for three weeks and legislates for the whole Church. Its membership is most distinguished and consists of leaders in every department of our national activities. It is the most influential religious gathering in America."

"This is very interesting," said the Doctor, "but I should like to ask this question. You state that your Church has had continuous existence from Apostolic days. Is it then the first or earliest Church?"

"That question needs a careful answer, Doctor," replied the Rector. "You will realize that the earliest organization has had a troubled history. Its indentity has not been lost but its unity has been shattered. The Episcopal Church is only one of several historic churches."

"It is too late tonight to begin on that," concluded the Major. "Let's save it until next week."

CHAPTER VIII.

THE HISTORY OF THE CHURCH.

When the Doctor reached the Rector's study the next week he saw upon the Rector's desk a long row of books.

"Look at them, Doctor," urged the Rector.

The Doctor selected one and began turning the pages.

"They seem to be histories," was his comment.

"They are," asserted the Rector. "They are histories of the Christian Church."

"Not very lively reading, Rector," suggested the Doctor.

"Perhaps not, unless one is interested. But they are very wholesome reading for the average man, if not for their details, at least for the enlarging of his notion as to the place and influence of the Church in the development of European civilization."

"They go back pretty far," said the Doctor. "Here is an account of a Church Council in the year 325 A. D."

"They go back farther than that. It is curious

that many people have a notion that Christianity has always had its present form of numerous religious sects. Many think that because they have heard their grandfathers tell of conditions in their childhood that they have penetrated into the past far enough to judge of conditions from the very beginning. That is not the case."

"Evidently not," admitted the Doctor. "We are going somewhat further back tonight, are we not?"

"We are indeed. And here come our fellow-students," said the Rector, greeting them.

The Judge and the Major entered together.

"Started yet, Rector?" asked the Major.

"The drive is not yet begun," answered the Doctor, "but here is the ammunition," and he pointed to the books.

"Is the ammunition dry?" asked the Major.

"Tolerably dry, Major," said the Rector, "but more useful on that account."

"Some old friends of mine here," said the Judge, picking up a volume. "It is a good thing to enlarge one's knowledge by an acquaintance with a few substantial books."

"Quite right, Judge," said the Major. "Even the Doctor does not erect the science of medicine by individual effort. You use the accumulated efforts of the past, do you not, Doctor?"

The Doctor smiled in assent.

"You do not understand the Episcopal Church, Doctor," began the Rector, "unless you understand its historical background. Anyone who believes that the Church of this generation, or of the past few generations, invented our ritual and our practices, and our officers, much as a new lodge invents its formularies, is quite mistaken. The Episcopal Church has a history of a thousand years previous to the time when religious denominations began to spring up."

"Is it the oldest church, then, Rector?" asked the Doctor.

"It is one part of the original Church, founded by Jesus Christ. There are other churches that have the same historic origin."

"I presume you mean the Roman Catholic?"

"Yes, and the great Greek Church, which is not Roman Catholic at all, and is the church of one hundred millions of people in the East, especially the Russians."

"Did the Episcopal Church spring from the Roman Catholic Church, Rector?" asked the Doctor.

"Not at all. Its roots are in the same past, but since the second century, our Anglican Communion has had distinct historic existence."

"Rector," interposed the Judge, " why not begin at the beginning and trace its history?"

"I shall be glad to do so. But first I must caution you on two points. You must not be confused by the question of names. The Episcopal Church as a continuous body has had various names in the past. The stream can be traced back through many political and social changes, in all of which were evolved new phases of history. And then again I must protest that I am not giving you merely present day theories about our origin, projected back into a shadowy past, but the verdict of reliable history, to be absolutely trusted in its general conclusions. This is not a belief, obscure and indistinct, but a great fact to which all reliable history bears testimony."

"I understand," said the Doctor, pointing to the books.

"In tracing the history of the Church I can give only the great main outlines, and that with special reference to the Church in England and our Church in America.

"Our Lord Jesus Christ founded an institution which he called His Church. It was a definite organization. It had a constitution, which we call the Faith. It had officers, Apostles, Bishops, Priests and Deacons. It had sources of spiritual power and life, called sacraments; it was to represent Him, and to do what He would do were He able to be on earth everywhere and for all time. St. Paul calls this Church 'Christ's Body,' so closely associated was it with Him. Its life began on Whitsunday at Jerusalem, in the year 29, ten days after our Lord left the earth.

"This organization was very small at first, but it had the power to grow and enlarge. The apostles consecrated successors, called bishops, to carry on the Church. The bishops ordained priests and deacons. The Church wrote its own history. We call it the New Testament. But there are numerous other historical documents which tell us of the growth of the organization.

"The Church thus founded spread about the Mediterranean Sea. By the year 100 A. D., it existed in Africa, Asia Minor, Greece, Italy and Gaul. Before the end of the second century it had been planted in the island of Britain. It was one great universal organization, holding a common faith, having the same ministry, administering the same sacraments, and preaching the Gospel of Jesus Christ.

"But as it grew it began to be influenced by the national customs and languages of the lands to which it extended. In the East the services were held in Greek and in the West in Latin. In various sections the Church used the local tongues.

"But it was one universal Church. The word universal is the same as the word Catholic. The Church was Catholic in the sense that it was universal. That is the sense in which we use the word in the Creed. You must not confuse this use of the word with the popular use in our day, when people mistakenly say Catholic, when they mean Roman Catholic. In these early centuries the use of the words Roman Catholic, was unknown. There was a branch of the Catholic or Universal Church in Rome, just as there was in Greece and Egypt and England.

"Naturally during the first three centuries the Church began, in various places, to assume a pronounced national character. In Greece, Greeks would be chosen to the ministry and in England the Britains would be chosen. These men would naturally share in the national life and aspirations of their lands.

"By the year 323 A. D., the Church Universal had grown so powerful throughout the great Roman Empire that Constantine the Emperor declared Christianity to be the authorized religion of the Empire.

"Under his direction a great Council was called at Nicea in Asia Minor. Here came together 318 bishops and other prelates representative of every part of the Universal Church.

"This Council set forth the Nicene Creed, as a somewhat more complete exposition of the Christian Faith than the Apostles' Creed. This Nicene Creed is in our Prayer Books and we use it every Sunday at the Service of the Holy Communion.

"But you must remember that great political and social changes were taking place at this time.

"There were bishops at every great center and in countless small cities. It was natural that the bishops of very large cities should have power which the other bishops did not have. They associated themselves with the political development of the time. So it came to pass that in two cities especially, Constantinople and Rome, the bishops began to assume a leadership among their fellows. By 500 A. D. the Bishops of both Constantinople and Rome had assumed power in the Church which brought disaster. In Rome this was the beginning of a tendency which later developed into the Papacy or the assumption of the Bishop of Rome of a position of authority over the whole Church.

"You must remember, however, that the Church in Rome was not at that time what it is today, but was still part of the Universal Church, in spite of these claims of its Bishops.

"These claims were resisted by the branch of the Church in Constantinople, and so serious did the conflict become that finally the Church in the East and the Church at Rome separated. This was in the year 1054. At this time Rome had succeeded in bringing all the churches in southern Europe under its sway. The Church of England alone remained beyond its uncontested authority. The Church of England, while acknowledging Rome as the metropolis of Christendom, and maintaining relations more or less obscure and vague with that metropolis, was nevertheless in no essential manner dependent for its existence upon Rome. The Church in England was complete in itself. In the meantime the churches about the southern shore of the Mediterranean and in Asia Minor had been destroyed by the invasion of the Turks. In 1054 the East and West separated and the Continental Church was broken into two parts. The Church in England retained its original standing. The year 1054 marks historically the separate existence of the branch of the Universal Church in Rome as distinctly the Roman Catholic Church.

"Let us see what was happening in England.

"The Church had been brought to England in the second century. It had its full organization there and was a part of the Universal Church, and was represented at the Council of Nicea in 325 A. D. This may be called the British or Celtic period of the Church in Britain, which later becomes known to us as the Church of England.

"In the fourth and fifth centuries the Angles, Saxons, and Jutes invaded England and drove the original inhabitants, the Celts, or Britains, with the Church, toward the west, into Ireland, Cornwall, and Wales. Thus Britain became heathen again after having had the Church for three centuries.

"Immediately the Church began an effort to convert these heathen invaders, and missionaries from the Celtic Church made their way back again among the Anglo-Saxons. This effort at conversion was reinforced by another effort which came from the continent of Europe. St. Augustine, with a band of followers, representing the same Universal Church of which the Celtic Church was a part, landed in Kent and came to Canterbury. There he found a church building which had not been destroyed by the invaders. This church building, called St. Martin's, still stands just as St. Augustine found it in 597 A. D., and is visited today by great throngs of people who see in it another witness to the historic continuity of the Church of England.

"After some controversy and conflict the efforts of Augustine and the efforts of the Celtic missionaries blended into one great structure in which the outlines of the Church of England as at present existing are clearly seen. The ancient British stream of Christianity and the stream from Rome through Augustine flowed together into the mighty river of the English Church, in the seventh century.

"This united Church preceded the united Kingdom, and by the efforts of the Church the united Kingdom was established.

"During this period the Church of England maintained an indefinite and unnecessary relationship with Rome, whose far more advanced political and social organization gave her an appearance of power and authority which overshadowed the English Church, struggling toward control of the conditions necessary to its continuance and well-being. But you must not forget that this was before the day in which Rome had acquired those later additions to which we object. At that time both the Church of England and the Church of Rome were conscious of being part of a greater unity, namely the Church Catholic, or the Church Universal.

"Up to the year 1066 the Church continued to grow strong, having preserved all the necessary functions by which it maintained its continuous existence from the Church of Apostolic days.

"In the year 1066 however, a great political change took place. William the Norman came to England from France and conquered the land. William the Norman was a Roman Catholic. That is to say, he owed allegiance to the Western Church in Europe which, having separated from the Eastern Church in 1054, now laid claim to the allegiance of all Christians in the West. England, because of its isolation, had been somewhat exempt from these pretensions. When William conquered the land, however, he proceeded to attempt to control the Church and to bring it into subjection to the Church of Rome. The Church of England resisted this vigorously and the next four hundred years of its history is a period of continual conflict against the aggressions of the Church of Rome. The rulers of the nation were often adherents of the Church of Rome however, and by their power put Roman Catholic officials in high places. History gives us many evidences of this struggle. The charter of English liberty, called *Magna Charta,* the parchment of which still exists in the British Museum in London, asserts as one of its principles, that the Church of England shall be forever free and inviolable. This struggle of the Church of England for independence might have continued much longer had it not been for the rise of an occasion in which the King of England rejected the authority of the Pope. This was the famous King Henry VIII. He was a Roman Catholic and a vicious man. I know that you have heard the myth that he founded the Church of England, but this is only a popular legend fostered by the Church of Rome to discredit the historical existence of the Church of England. King Henry VIII wished to divorce his wife, for which he asked permission from the Pope. The Pope refused to give him permission and he rejected the Pope's authority. When the King turned against the power of the Church of Rome in England, the Church of England found its opportunity to drive out all Roman control, and in 1534 the legal steps were taken which made it impossible for the Church of Rome ever again to regain any control over the Church of England. This was called the period of the Reformation. From that time to the present day the Church of England has retained its rights and its property with only two brief struggles, one against the power of Queen Mary, and the other against Oliver Cromwell and his puritans. Thus the Church of England can trace its existence from this present year back through all the troublous times of the Reformation, back through the period of Roman influence, back into the clearer days of the Anglo-Saxons, back past the invasion of England by the Anglo-Saxons, back through the Celtic Church to the planting of the Church in Britain in the second century, a branch of the Apostolic Church.

"The Episcopal Church in the United States grew directly out of the Church of England and whatever historic spiritual authority has resided within the Church of England is the possession of the Episcopal Church in America. The first services in this country were held in Jamestown in 1607 by Robert Hunt, the chaplain who came over with Captain John Smith on his memorable voyage. This was thirteen years before the Pilgrims landed at Plymouth. Later many clergymen of the Church of England came to the Colonies and many of our parishes in the eastern cities are several hundred years old."

"I have visited some of the old churches," said the Doctor.

"We have many parishes of early Colonial days. Trinity Church in New York city, was organized in 1697. The first parish in Boston was organized even earlier, in 1686. It gives one a sense of the age of our Church to visit these parishes founded before the Revolution. But I had a more impressive experience once. I was in Chester, in England, and one Sunday evening went to service in a little church which I had discovered almost by chance. I found the parish in the midst of an anniversary service, celebrating, as I now remember, the 1237th year of its organization. Think of it! It gave me a thrill to realize that the great spiritual household, of which my parish was a part, had ministered on that spot for so many years. I learned that the very building in which I sat was erected in the eleventh century. This made me realize that our American Episcopal Church was yet young, and that its strength was not yet tried; that there were before it glorious years of growth and struggle; that it had a mission to our nation not yet discharged; that in God's time, if it persevered, it would bring to our land the untold blessings of a firm faith and the blessings of countless treasures of loving service in the name of Christ. We grow impatient Doctor, at our slow progress, but we must realize that the Church will ultimately grow into a mighty and all-prevailing Kingdom, if it holds fast, with persevering stewardship, the riches of life and faith, which have been committed to its keeping."

CHAPTER IX.

THE BACKGROUND OF WORSHIP.

The four friends had gathered as usual about the fire in the Rector's study. The Doctor was examining a picture of an English Cathedral hung above the stone mantle.

"A great building," was his comment. "They make our modern churches seem commonplace."

"Many of them are so," said the Judge. "But we must not judge entirely by appearances. Our own church is very simple and yet we love it. Churchmen have a deep sense of appreciation of the sacredness of the church structure."

"You say Churchmen, Judge," declared the Doctor. "Do you mean Episcopalians?"

"I do." answered the Judge. "I prefer the word Churchmen, however. For several centuries this word has been used to designate those who adhere to the historic Church. You need only consult the Century Dictionary if you ask authority for this use of the word."

The Rector walked to his bookcase and drew

out the volume. Turning to the word 'Churchman' he read—

"'Churchman—specifically, a member of the Church of England as distinguished from a dissenter; in the United States, a member of the Protestant Episcopal Church, as distinguished from a member of any other Church.'"

"That appears to be sufficient authority," admitted the Doctor. "I have noticed that Churchmen, to use the word, are very loyal to their Church. They seldom desert it. They seem to love the very building."

"Quite true," the Judge assured him. "And every parish church has a peculiar glory which we see through all its simplicity."

"Your church is quite plain in its appointments but it has an atmosphere that recalls sacred things," added the Doctor.

"The parish church is a symbol of the complete riches of the historic Church," continued the Judge. "We feel ourselves to be not only in the presence of that particular set of familiar associations, but in the full current of the Church's life throughout all the centuries."

"I never quite realized that," asserted the Doctor. "The building itself has never meant much more to me than a convenient place in which to assemble the people. The service was merely a convenient method of holding a religious exercise for the congregation."

"You are missing all the background of it, Doctor," declared the Rector. "You are missing all the sense of contact with the richness of the Church's life for a thousand years. That is perhaps the hardest thing to create in the minds of the people, but once formed it never loses its power and charm."

Here the Major interrupted.

"Last summer I went to Concord, Massachusetts, and visited the home of Louisa M. Alcott. Have you ever been there, Doctor?"

"Several times. Charming place."

"But why so fascinating?" urged the Major. "A very simple house, with no pretense at originality in design or construction. There are hundreds of houses like it in New England. Why do multitudes visit it every year?"

"You know as well as I do, Major," affirmed the Doctor. "Miss Alcott, through her books, has made it live in the imaginations of countless thousands of young people."

"You are right. It has an historical background. Imagination has elevated it into a shrine. It is the same with the Church."

"How is that the case with your parish church which has never had any such illuminating interpreter as the old Alcott house had?" and he gave an apologetic look toward the Rector. "Has it, Rector?" he concluded.

"The parish church," began the Rector, "is illumined and transformed by the whole of which it is a very small part. When I enter it I feel that it is part of a great structure that for nearly nineteen centuries has been enriching the world. The church suggests to me all these greater and remote things."

"Our church is but a feeble reflection of all this treasure, but imagination, the most wonderful gift by which the commonplace is transformed into the glorious, imagination begins to pour the treasure of the past into the present.

"When I minister within the sacred walls of our church, I feel myself to be not only in the presence of the few who are gathered there, but of the countless throngs who have assembled throughout the centuries to share in the same service, part of the same historic Church, members of Christ in the same household. I think of the saints and martyrs who proclaimed the same faith which our congregation proclaims. I think of the ancient Celtic people who, while the Romans were still in England, in their rude structures knelt before the altar to partake of the Bread of Life, administered by a priest, of the same historic priesthood in which I have a part. I think of the later Anglo-Saxon Christians, our ancestors, converted and baptized by their priests and erecting their altars to God. I think of the later congregations in Norman times, assembling in their cathedrals and giving praise to God. And I think of the Church of today, spread abroad to every corner of the earth where the English language is spoken. On every Sunday, aye, on nearly every day of the year, 'from the rising of the sun to the going down thereof'—a mighty chorus of prayer and praise and sacrifice encircles the globe, in the worship of God, from congregations of Churchmen, led by priests and using the Book of Common Prayer. We are but a single link in a great chain of worship that never ceases. We of the Episcopal Church feel that. We know we are not alone.

"One of the most impressive experiences of my life was at the great Albert Hall, in London, where ten thousand Churchmen, gathered from every land, from England and America, from Australia, from Japan and China, and from the isles of the sea, arose, and with one voice recited the Apostles' Creed. It made me realize that when our little congregation asserts its faith, it is but part of a vast multitude, millions upon millions of people, who, in every part of the earth, are proclaiming their faith in God and Christ and their love for men."

"I shall remember that when we say the Creed next Sunday," declared the Judge. "It seems a feeble exercise when one thinks of it as merely an individual expression, but it is a mighty proclamation when millions unite to assert its everlasting truth."

"Again," continued the Rector, "the little church begins, under the powerful influence of imagination, to sink into the shadow, and out into the sunlight of my mind comes the majestic outline of the great Cathedral, such as the one you were looking at, Doctor. I am no longer in the seclusion of my parish with only its simple structure, but in the vast stretches of those historic buildings, which are spiritually as much our possession as our own church. Our church is not the limit of our ecclesiastical associations and is not intended to confine our thoughts to its own limitations, but it serves as a window through which appears the greater vision which is really ours. For the mighty structures of old, although they are confined to a place, have in them unbounded wealth of association which our people may absorb and make their own. Even as a book, read by one's fireside, may open up a world in which men live and act, and in whose lives and loves, thoughts and actions, we may become so absorbed that we really feel part of that world, so that we laugh and cry with them; even so the parish church is but a book, the reading of which places us in the larger world of the Church's possessions. I reach out, in thought, to all the greater places, which I may call my own as completely as do those who live in sight of their walls; I am in the Cathedral, whose tall pillars support the majestic arches; in the vista of the nave I see the priceless windows, constructed by the loving hands of consecrated artists. The vast spaces suggest the glory of the Heavenly places. The rich toned organ pours forth its melodies. The long procession of white vested choristers wends its way through nave to choir, followed by richly robed priests, of the same ministry as my own. On they go to the great Altar and then I hear the familiar words carried to every heart of the kneeling congregation. I am not isolated with only my people, but we are all together in the splendor of the worship of the Church of all the centuries. Every word, every phrase, every vestment, every article of furniture, every hymn, every association and custom of our worship, is but a reflection of a glorious past in which the countless worshippers have upbuilded an enduring structure which shelters us in its beneficence. And all is charged, not alone with the richness of man's spiritual expression, but with the very presence of God."

"Do all your people feel that, Rector?" asked the Doctor quietly.

"Perhaps not, but they may, if they will but surrender themselves to the conviction that they are a part of a great Church that for nineteen hundred years has been bringing men to God and creating a structure whose riches are theirs. To isolate the parish church from its background, to insulate it from the great body of which it is a part, is to impoverish it."

"But is there not danger of forgetting the needs of the present under the fascination of the past?" asked the Doctor. "Imagination may create an unreal world, while the problems of the present are pressing upon us."

"No indeed, Doctor. You will realize that I am endeavoring to illumine the worship. The work of the Church is to bring the reality of God and His law and love, and His revelation in Christ, to the lives and hearts of men. The worship is to enrich the life and make it capable of the best service. But it is only when one realizes that the spiritual nature of man must be strengthened in order that his life may be made useful and happy, and free from sin, that one realizes that the spiritual riches of the past must be appropriated. Our worship does this. We are building upward but our foundation must be secure. We shall never have a powerfully developed people unless the past furnishes them with its best."

"Has not the Church in times past given man some of his most cherished spiritual possessions expressed in great artistic creations?" asked the Judge.

"It has. Our Church, throughout its long history, has been a workshop in which the most venerated of the creations of the past have been forged. And this conviction creeps over me in the service, too. I long to feel that the Church in the present may be as abundantly powerful in creating those spiritual structures by which men are enriched as the Church in the past has been.

"I think of the ways in which the consecrated human spirit has expressed itself for the glory of God and the service of men. The great Cathedrals of England are an example of what I mean. They are ours as much as Shakespeare is ours. They are not the result of the efforts of school trained architects, assisted by construction companies. Many of them were a hundred years in building. They arose from the consecrated effort of religious people. New designs were evolved from a growing appreciation of the laws of structure, and of the beauty of line and proportion. Whole populations found a means of spiritual expression in working upon the growing temple. Workers in stone skillfully formed the great blocks, and many a man spent his life with his hammer and chisel in giving beauty to the walls. Workers in metal were ministers of beauty and strength. Artificers wrought the wonders of glass. And today they stand not only for us to admire, but they stand to instruct us in appreciation of the wonders of the human spirit, when consecrated to noblest service. They are a gospel in stone, a gospel of the divine in man. And I rejoice to worship in our Church because it is part of that stream of Christian power in which those great Cathedrals were upbuilded to the glory of God.

"I love to think, when I read the Bible to the people, that not only did the Church preserve the Bible, but it translated the Bible from its original tongues and placed it before the world. Within the Church also have arisen the countless scholars, who, by devotion and study, have bequeathed to all Christendom the most valuable possessions of Christian scholarship. Every Christian is indebted to them.

"I might enlarge upon these things, Doctor, but I feel that one evening would not suffice to rehearse even a small portion of them.

"Back into the past stretches the long corridor of our Church's life. Through one century after another it extends, even until it approaches that Figure who gave it life and being. Every century has contributed its part. Art, architecture, music, literature and learning, have all been humble handmaids to the historic Church. They have contributed to its growth and power, to its beauty and to its contact with the spiritual aspirations of the people.

"I cannot undervalue all this history. It has meant too much to the world. And today I rejoice that I am serving a Church which has brought such treasures to men. I rejoice that I can bring to my people a vision of the past which will fill their minds with images never to be forgotten, a vision of the wondrous ways in which men consecrated to God have given expression to the beauties of His Kingdom."

The Rector ceased. All kept silent for a while. Finally the Doctor asked the question, "Do you try to make your people feel all this when they go to church?"

"Not only when they go to church, Doctor, but always. Their Christian life and their share in the Kingdom is not confined to the hour at church. That serves but to recall and keep fresh their constant relation to God, in His Church. They should feel, at home and at work, that they share in God's Kingdom on earth. But it is more powerfully felt at church. Do not misunderstand me. It is not for itself that we try to enlarge the vision and arouse the imagination. We do so because it quickens the spiritual impulse, and when the spiritual impulse is quickened it arouses the desire not only to share in the Kingdom but to serve it. And then comes the desire to work and to serve men in this world.

"This means that our spiritual nature must find, under the guidance of the Church today, its method of creative expression. The Church today will not create architecture and be satisfied with that. It will not create music or art and rejoice in that. That day has passed. We shall indeed perpetuate in architecture, art, and music, the splendors of the past, and they may develop under the cultivation of centuries. But this great historic Church must find in this century its method of expression and must not merely reproduce the past."

"And what do you think the contribution of the Church will be, in this century?" asked the Doctor.

"It is too early to determine, Doctor," admitted the Rector. "But there are several strong tendencies any one of which may result in the Church's contribution to the spiritual wealth of the age. One of them may be called the effort of the Church to supply the elements that are missing in our democracy, and without which democracy will fail, and they are the elements of unselfishness and righteousness. Or it may be that the Church will find its highest mission to be the social uplift of humanity—so that justice may prevail in our land. Or it may be that the Episcopal Church may find that its adherence to its past and to its faith will be the moving power under which divided and distracted Christendom will be guided to reunion and strength. Or it may be that the Church's devotion to the services of the Altar, according to Christ's own direction, will be the central influence by which the people will be led from godlessness, from fads and fancies in religion, to the contemplation and worship and discipleship of the Christ crucified for man, and thus restore to wavering religions their central strength. I do not know. But I do know that if men feel the glory of its past, they will be more eager to maintain its glory in the future. And when, in God's time, there emerges the crowning work of the Church in this century they will rejoice that they had their share in it."

"And if I wish to have a share in it what should I do?" asked the Doctor.

"You should become part of it. Half hearted allegiance or unwillingness to let all the riches of the Church possess you will avail nothing. Be loyal. Learn of the Church's past, and the glory of it. Learn of its present, its needs and struggles. Do not stand afar off and pretend to judge of the Church, and perhaps condemn it, or ignore it, but share in its work and hopes and ideals. Better be a toiler in the Church than one indifferent or critical. Then live this life, whole-heartedly. Learn what discipleship in Christ means. For the Church is nothing apart from Him. Share its faith and be true to Him. Make it a matter of practical effort to absorb all that the Church has, not an occasional or partial element of it. Be whole-hearted in it, and then you will be a worthy servant of your Master."

CHAPTER X.

THE CHRISTIAN YEAR.

"I WENT to church again last Sunday," began the Doctor as the group assembled about the cheery fire.

"Always welcome," said the Judge. "How does it impress you, now?"

"It is beginning to seem quite the normal thing to do. The service means something to me and I believe that I have forgotten to feel that it was once quite formal."

"Are you getting accustomed to the Prayer Book, Doctor?" asked the Judge.

"Somewhat. But I do have a little difficulty in finding the places."

"Let me give you a suggestion. In such an important matter a little attention to the Prayer Book is worth while. It is not as complex as you imagine. I would advise you, and everyone who has any difficulty, to sit down quietly at home and to turn over the pages and read the headings and also the directions printed in small type, called *rubrics*.

"Many of the services are occasional such as the Service of Baptism. The customary services are *Morning and Evening Prayer*, from page 1 to 29, *The Litany* from page 30 to 36 and the *Service of Holy Communion* from page 221 to 243. If you read those pages carefully you will find it easy to follow the service."

"But you stated some time ago that while the structure of the service was the same, the substance of it changed from Sunday to Sunday. How may one find the parts that change?"

"*Morning Prayer* has four variable parts: the opening sentences, all of which are printed on pages 1 to 3, but only two or three of which are used at any service; the Psalms, which are selected from the Book of Psalms printed on pages 329 to 508, and which are announced; the Lessons from the Bible, read by the Minister; and the Chants, or Canticles, which are used after the lessons.

"In the *Service of Holy Communion* there is but one variable part, that which we call the Collect, Epistle and Gospel. Beginning on page 52 you will find printed, in succession, a Collect, Epistle and Gospel for every Sunday and Holy Day of the year. To find these requires a little more practice, since you must know what Sunday or Holy Day is being observed, and where on these pages the Collect, Epistle and Gospel are to be found. In our church there is a bulletin board, at the top of which is posted the name of the Sunday or Holy Day, and under which is given the page in the Prayer Book on which the Collect, Epistle and Gospel are to be found."

"What is the Collect?" asked the Doctor.

"The Collect is an ancient name for a Prayer. The Epistle is a portion of one of the Epistles of the New Testament, and the Gospel is a portion of one of the four Gospels. They are arranged to set forth the great facts in our Lord's life and teaching.

"You must remember, Doctor, that the Episcopal Church observes the Christian Year. There are eight seasons, seven of which set forth the facts of our Lord's life, and one sets forth His teaching.

"This is a part of the educational effort of the Church. It also provides a method that is sympathetic with the instinct of men to have times and seasons in which to enjoy the various phases of human experience."

"How old is this arrangement?" asked the Doctor.

"It began with the origin of Christianity but it has developed during the centuries. Almost every religious body pays it a tribute by observing some portion of the Christian year. For example, the Christian world observes Christmas and Easter. They are the great mountain peaks in the range of Christian observance practiced by the historic Churches."

"I know, of course, the general meaning of the observance of Christmas and Easter. What are the other seasons?"

"The Christian year begins near December first with a season of four weeks, called Advent. The word 'advent' means coming. Look on page 52 of the Prayer Book and you will find the title of the first Sunday of the Christian year, 'The First Sunday in Advent.' In this season the Church sets forth the truth and facts of the expectation of our Lord's first and second coming to earth.

"This is followed, naturally, by the presentation of the fact of His first coming, in the Christmas season. (Prayer Book, page 58.) This season lasts twelve days.

"It is followed by the Epiphany season which begins January 6th. (Prayer Book, page 69.) The word Epiphany means a showing forth, or manifestation, and in this season the Church emphasizes the fact that Jesus Christ came to be the Saviour, not of the Jews only, but of all people.

"Epiphany is followed by Lent which is a season of prayer and fasting. (Prayer Book, page 86). Within the season of Lent and especially toward its close, as on Good Friday, the Church sets forth the facts of our Lord's death upon the Cross. (Page 118.)

"Lent is followed by Easter. (Page 125.) It is a strange fact that many churches observe Easter but do not observe Good Friday which precedes it. The Easter message completes the Good Friday message. It is a strangely inconsistent and spiritually confusing thing to keep Easter and pay no attention to Good Friday. But the observance of Good Friday is increasing.

"The Easter season lasts forty days, the time our Lord remained on earth after the Resurrection, and is followed by the Ascension season, beginning with Ascension Day, which always falls upon a Thursday. At this time the Church commemorates our Lord's Ascension into Heaven. This season lasts ten days. (Page 140.)

"Ascension-tide is followed by Whitsunday, always a Sunday. This day is commemorated as the day on which the Holy Spirit descended upon the Apostles. This is the birthday of the Christian Church. (Page 143.)

"These seven seasons occupy about six months of the year.

"Whitsunday is followed by the Trinity season, which lasts about six months. (Prayer Book, page 148, on.) During this season the Church sets forth our Lord's teaching."

"What is the advantage of the Christian year?" asked the Doctor.

"There are many advantages. In the first place it secures attention, in proper order, to the great truths of Christianity. It is not haphazard. This orderly progression of the presentation of the facts of our Lord's life is impressive and instructive.

"Again, it provides variety. Every Sunday has its burden of truth and power. The colors, the hymns, the sermon, all blend to give it distinctiveness."

"I can go into any Episcopal Church," said the Judge, "and determine the season almost at once."

"Not only that, Judge," urged the Rector, "but the Church throughout the world is using practically the same service on any Sunday. For you must remember, Doctor, that the Christian year is not a device of the Episcopal Church, but it is a great historical expression of the consciousness of the relation of times and seasons to our vital experiences."

"But is it a matter of Sunday alone?"

"Not at all. All time, week days and Sundays, is included. One season merges into another. There are many week days which the Church observes. One who gets the full sense of the beauty of the Christian year becomes conscious of the sacred nature of time, irrespective of any arrangement of days. The hard and fast difference between Sundays and week days is a modern notion, which tends to eliminate the exercise of religious feeling or practice from six days of the week. The Christian year corrects this misconception."

"What about Lent? Do you not become more strict in Lent?"

"In a certain way, yes," admitted the Rector.

"I do not see why a Christian should be more strict in Lent. It seems to me to be somewhat formal to observe Lent."

"I am afraid, Doctor, that you measure the Church by one set of standards and other activities by a different set."

"What do you mean by that?" asked the Doctor.

"Merely this. The whole world applies the principle of Lent to its affairs. You seem to affirm that to have a special time to pay attention to some human need is formal. But Lent is merely an educational and disciplinary season.

You apply it in a score of ways, as I said. For example, you believe in education."

"Surely," said the Doctor.

"But do you not set certain hours and certain seasons for your child's education? By common consent the child goes to school during the middle of the day and for about ten months of the year."

"That is a necessary arrangement," urged the Doctor.

"So is Lent! The Church ministers to thousands of people, even as the schools do. So it must arrange times and seasons. Lent is such an arrangement."

"I understand so far," admitted the Doctor, "but why have special religious exercises and habits for so short a time and not for the whole year?"

"You take a vacation, do you not, Doctor?"

"Yes, when I can."

"It's a good thing for you, is it not? If so, why not make the whole year a vacation? You play golf, do you not?" continued the Rector without waiting for a reply. "It is a fine exercise. Why not play all the time? You read medical books. Why not spend your whole day at it?

"You misunderstand Lent, Doctor. The average man is so absorbed with duties and social affairs that he would fail to pay proper attention to his own individual needs were he never to have the direction of the Church in arranging a time, a season.

"Lent is a time for discipline, for paying attention to the needs of one's own soul, for determining who is master, the man or his appetites. It is a time when he foregoes some of his usual but unnecessary occupations and social engagements, and turns his thoughts to matters of his eternal welfare. His sacrifices, his abstinence from purely social affairs, are merely an effort toward disengaging himself from distracting conditions. In the time thus gained, he weighs his life according to its larger relations. He does not give up the theatre because the theatre is necessarily wrong, but because he wishes to clear life of its less important activities, in favor of discipline. He does it for the same reason that the man with an important work to do must clear away the obstructing engagements.

"Then, in the time thus gained and with the use of the mental attention thus secured, he tries to upbuild spiritual strength.

"There are many people, Doctor, who scarcely dare to face their own spiritual condition and life's deepest meaning and responsibilities.

They would smother the truth by a constant round of petty activities and attentions which keep the more serious duties and responsibilities from them. They live on a kind of excitement, or at least with mind centered on temporal and passing things. To those who have such a tendency Lent comes as a time of sober reflection, renewed effort at righteousness, and refreshed souls.

"I know that some people think of it as a time of gloom and joylessness and despondency. That is a total misunderstanding of it. One does not give up his usual recreation merely to irritate himself. It is a matter of discipline and self-control. And it makes Lent a time of reinvigoration and refreshment. There is underneath the observance of Lent a profound joy in the fact that one is master of his environment and habits.

"This is a work-a-day world, Doctor. You practice many months in the year, but once in a while you go into a hospital to attend clinics and keep up with your profession. So the member of the Church finds work within and without the Church. He must serve his fellow men. But a time comes when he must sound his own depths and make sure that his own life and habits are not earth-bound. Lent provides this opportunity. It is as essential to man's spiritual health, as a vacation is to his physical refreshment."

"When our boys went to war, Doctor," put in the Major, "they were first sent to training camps, not only to be schooled but to be hardened by the process. They were not only to be drilled but to be made 'fit.' As I understand it, Lent is the time for training in life's necessary discipline. By it one determines, too, whether the non-essentials have actually become essentials in life. Sacrifice is a great source of strength."

"Well said, Major," commended the Judge. "I look forward to Lent as I would to a day in the woods, after a confused and distracted life in the midst of the noise of a city It gives me a chance to know myself."

"But are not its requirements arbitrary?" asked the Doctor.

"Not arbitrary in the Episcopal Church. That is the last word to use about Lent. Lent is a privilege. While the Church suggests certain methods, such as abstaining from usual amusements and social affairs, and also urges moderation in eating and even enjoins fasting, the Church imposes Lent on no one. Here again is the liberty within the Church emphasized. But more important than what it suggests as Lenten discipline, is what it suggests as Lenten exercises; greater fidelity to the habit of prayer, more frequent communions, more religious reading, greater care in upbuilding religious habits and more concern for absolute righteousness. But each member of the Church is free to do as he wills."

"Fasting is a good practice," said the Doctor. "It contributes to health and strength if moderately practiced."

"Moderation is an excellent virtue in all things," added the Judge.

"Is not Lent a sort of revival?" asked the Major.

"It might be so considered. But the Episcopal Church does not stress the emotional value in religion to the exclusion of the other values. The Church tries to care for the child as the gardener cares for the flower. He does not attempt to change a seed into a flower by forced methods. No, he plants the seed, waters the growing plant, cares for it, keeps it free from insect enemies, and finally the flower is the result.

"So the Church enfolds the child or even the adult and encourages the growing plant of spirituality to grow and become the flower. The child is instructed, cared for, put into the sunshine of God's love, kept free from sinful environments, nourished with truth, and directed to worship and service. Such a child grows normally into his Christian stature.

"At times, indeed, conversion becomes a necessity. Conversion means a turning about. A man on the wrong road must be faced about. But every faculty must be engaged in the process, not feeling alone. Feeling may encourage the movement, but conversion implies a different mental attitude, an appreciation of the real values of life, and it must be made sure by the establishing of the man in a completely new spiritual environment. He must be taught the Faith, must be rooted in new habits and he must allow his whole being to reinforce those resolutions which may have been primarily aroused by his feelings only. There is nothing that vanishes so quickly as overstrained feeling.

"Lent serves to blend feeling, faith, knowledge, and purpose, in an effective stimulus toward righteousness. In that sense it is a revival."

"Do you not think that it requires a good deal of courage for the Episcopal Church to remain steadfast in its methods, and loyal to its convictions, when it has so much opposition or indifference to overcome, and when those methods seem the most difficult way of attracting great numbers of people to the Church?" asked the Doctor.

"It has required courage, and loyalty, and steadfastness. But the Church has its convictions. It is sure that it must be true to itself and not weaken its convictions to draw the crowds. The Church is sure of its mission, and confident of the final outcome. The Church believes that vast numbers of people will ultimately find in its presentation of the Christian religion a deep and abiding satisfaction that will repay the Church for its efforts.

"And this conviction seems to be confirmed by the growth of the Church in the last generation. It is growing in numbers at a greater rate than the population is increasing in our land.

"Where it has been long established, as in the Eastern states, it has acquired a power and influence out of all proportion to its numbers. In New York city alone it has over one hundred parishes. In the West it is becoming very strong, especially in large centers of population.

"Nor must we fail to take into consideration the power and influence of the larger spiritual Household of which we are a part.

"The Anglican Communion, which includes

the Church of England, the Episcopal Church in America, and the Church of England in her provinces, and all the missionary jurisdictions, numbers about thirty-five million communicants. We are a large company.

"Inspired by the conquests of the past, sure of the Rock on which it is founded, certain of its divine origin, the Church faces, without fear, the years of labor in which it must uphold the banners of faith and righteousness, that the Kingdom of God may ultimately prevail on the earth."

CHAPTER XI.

THE CHURCH AND MEN OF TODAY.

"It seems that the Episcopal Church is an inexhaustible subject for study," said the Doctor when the little group next assembled in the Rector's library.

"It is," replied the Rector. "History, architecture, art, as well as scripture, theology and literature, are intermingled in its structure."

"Why have not all your people the benefit of such conferences as these?" asked the Doctor.

"They might have if they had the desire and would give me the opportunity. But many people hesitate to talk to the minister plainly about these things because they feel that he would misjudge them, and perhaps rebuke them for their opinions. That is not the case. It has been my experience that my men by plain talk have taught me as much as I have taught them. Many men have hold of vital truths. All they need is to have such truths adjusted to the whole system of religious truth so that they will be seen in proper perspective."

"Why is it that many men do not go to church, Rector?" asked the Doctor seriously.

"You have asked a large question, Doctor, and one to which I have given much thought. If you will be patient with me I shall give you my conclusions on the subject."

"We have the whole evening," put in the Judge.

"It has been my experience," began the Rector, "that many men, with honest conviction, living honest lives, have not found themselves in accord with the presentation of religion in their own community. They have felt that the various churches did not understand the spirit of this day, that they did not appreciate the real good, nor discriminate in their denunciations of worldwide practices and recreations. It has been impossible for some men to give their wholehearted devotion to churches, because they disagree with some of their points of view. They have been placed in the dilemma of either refraining from strict personal allegiance, or of appearing to approve of that which they in their hearts could not accept and in their lives did not care to practice. Such men have honestly preferred to support the church with contributions, as a tribute to the church's high purpose, but to withhold any personal allegiance, as being the most honorable thing to do in view of their personal convictions.

"There are others who, having no difficulties, nevertheless dismiss the church from their lives by reason of the pressure of other interests. They theoretically uphold the ideal of righteousness, which they conceive to be the main contention of churches, and they approve of churches, as useful agents in maintaining standards of right conduct, but they give no immediate personal allegiance to any church.

"Again there are those who believe that there are substitutes for organized Christianity. They find in lodges strong moral teaching and they find in social service the opportunity for personal endeavor. They believe themselves exempted from church affiliation. The church, so they believe, has nothing for them which they are not already receiving. This is a natural conclusion if the church is considered as a religious lodge with a sermon attached. But it shows a misapprehension of the purpose of the church.

"Again there are many men, yet young, who in their youth were subject to a discipline, often by parental authority, in Sunday school and church, which was distasteful and joyless. Not only were they taught doctrines against which in later years they rebelled, but they were compelled to practices from which later they gladly escaped. Their freedom was pleasant to them. But they have carried to maturity a sense of reaction against the restrictions of their youth, and at the same time they have retained a false notion of what religion expects of them and a false idea of what they must accept in the name of religion. They look with respect upon their former condition but with no eagerness to renew it.

"Again there are many men who have had no particular religious experience or training, who distrust the church because of the prevailing notion that the churches are teaching and practicing meagre and joyless doctrines and habits. They have not been attracted by the general atmosphere surrounding religious worship. As a matter of fact they have been too ready to listen to criticisms of the church in order to justify their own aloofness.

"Again there are men who believe that they are not in the proper frame of mind to accept religion in its organized bodies. They honestly believe that they are not good enough, or that they have not had any particular religious experience. They see organized Christianity holding revivals and otherwise emphasizing the emotional nature of religious experience and they realize that such an experience is foreign to their nature.

"Again there are others who hold intellectual opinions which they take for granted are not approved by the churches. Men have difficulties about the Bible, about the doctrines of future punishment, and about scientific truths, which, they assume, would bar them from membership in the churches.

"With men of such condition of mind and temperament I have a real sympathy. I honor them for the integrity of their purpose. Without doubt there is much justification for their attitude and it would be unnatural for them to think otherwise. For the churches have not been without fault in these matters and have been responsible for such conditions. But they are emerging from the ancient tyranny and from the inadequate presentations to which their zeal prompted them and are enlarging the bounds of their sympathy.

"And of course there are men who have shrunk to lives of worldliness and sinfulness. Naturally they have no concern for the church. But it would be a most grievous error in judgment to assume that any large percent of non-churchgoers are of this class."

"Do you believe," asked the Judge, as the

Rector paused, "that the church will again secure the allegiance of the majority of men?"

"It has already begun to do so, Judge," was the firm reply. "I believe that the church is adjusting itself to the temper of the day, and that men in large numbers are becoming interested in its new life and vision. I speak with absolute confidence when I say that the Episcopal Church in America has a most reassuring message to the men of this day. In its practices and teachings, in its expectations and in its loyalties the Church is sympathetic to the needs and conditions of modern life. Especially can it say to the men who are troubled by the difficulties mentioned above, that the Church respects those difficulties, because they express the attitude of right thinking and honorable men. Personally, I believe that the reluctance of men to assent to the persuasion of the churches has been valuable in compelling the Church to grow to the measure and stature of those whose support and allegiance it seeks. The Episcopal Church will neither dishonor itself nor belittle the men whom it attempts to serve, by abandoning a single fundamental religious truth, but it does assert that those fundamental truths do not afford any real basis for such attitudes as have been described, and that its whole temper, its whole atmosphere, its traditional practices, its expectations, are such that reluctant men may find a true home and intellectual and spiritual satisfaction within its borders."

"In what respect, Rector, has the Episcopal Church a special message to men today?" asked the Doctor.

"In the first place, Doctor, the Episcopal Church is holding fast to the fundamentals of the Christian faith. Men today respect convictions. They are tired of the guesses and the surmises and the frothy imaginings and the cheap sensationalism of those who under the pretense of liberty to believe what one likes, are offering often trifling substitutes for the sound and tried conclusions of universal Christendom. Men do not want religion to be belittled and reduced to mere amiability. Life, death, sin, and sorrow, loom too large in human affairs for men to be indifferent to the fundamental truth of God about these things. The Episcopal Church presents the Gospel of Christ as a whole, and the Christian faith as a whole, and not in such fragments as may please the hearer. It is the Church of great *affirmations.*

"Again, the Episcopal Church is not burdened by the religious idiosyncrasies and eccentricities that have clouded religious truth ever since men began to form the countless sects. I have not the least doubt in the world that many men confuse the Christian faith with crude and obscure notions which they learned in childhood and have never outgrown. Recently a man said to me that he thought that if one belonged to a church he had to believe literally every word in the Bible, including the statements that the world was made in six days. The Bible is the Word of God, I assuredly maintain, and the expression of God's revelation to men, and a spiritual, religious and moral food and stimulus, but it has its human framework and the limitations of any revelation of God through human instruments. To believe as that man believed is to make the Bible a book of magic, or an idol. The Episcopal Church teaches the Bible truth but it demands the use of reason and of spiritual appreciation in gathering the central truths from the Bible. Upon its members it imposes no obligation whatever to assent to any theory as to how the Bible is the word of God, but the Church teaches the Bible truth and tries to enrich the lives of its people by the message of God therein.

"It is not necessary to hold a *theory* about the Bible. The Church has gleaned the fundamental religious truths from it and interprets them to the people. The Episcopal Church gives full intellectual freedom to its members.

"And this is another reason why the Episcopal Church is so satisfying to men of this day. There was a time when Christianity seemed to be committed to the denial of the scientific discoveries of the day, such as, for example, the principle of evolution. Many religious bodies adhere to that denial. But the Episcopal Church has grown in its intellectual sympathies with the scientific advances of the day, and it encourages the fullest possible use of the human intellect in its discovery of truth.

"Again, the Episcopal Church is committed to the principle of moral freedom. The Church is not the accuser and judge of the people, but their advocate and friend. The Church directs its effort toward forming sound judgment and spiritual insight in the people, and toward setting forth the moral and religious principles by which life must be controlled. But the Episcopal Church does not erect a set of rules governing conduct and bind the people to them. In this land there are several things that some churches have attacked with vehemence, such as card playing, dancing and the theatre. The Episcopal Church sets forth the moral principles by which conduct must be guided and then permits its people to apply these principles to all conduct, even such things as dancing and theatre going. Almost any permissible thing may be abused, but its proper use is not therefore to be prohibited.

"Again, the Episcopal Church respects the individuality and personality of men. The Church does not try to reduce every life to some commonplace sameness of experience and interest, but tries to encourage every life to enlarge and expand to its own destiny. Men differ in temperament, habits, environment. Some enjoy the intellectual aspects of Christianity, some the emotional, some the philanthropic. To attempt to recreate each temperament and to have some identical mediocrity is folly. The Church does not expect it. The Church realizes that some men want to *know,* some want to *feel,* some want to *act.* The Church ministers to each type and respects it. Some men have never experienced conversion, and have no profound emotions. But the Church is comprehensive and asks those of honest purpose to come within the sphere of its life and teaching, and to serve God with their gifts, whatsoever they may be. At the same time, the Church endeavors to cultivate the neglected portions of their nature, to bring to them an appreciation of all the elements of a well rounded Christian experience, fortified by a reasonable faith.

"Again the Episcopal Church makes no man a hypocrite. A man may be a hypocrite by nature, but the Church does not make him one. I mean that the Church does not exact a profession from its members by which they later may be judged. The Church is not the judge but the friend.

"As a friend the Church is sympathetic. This sympathy extends to people in every circumstance of life and of every condition of heart. The Church desires to destroy sin but to save the sinner. Consequently the doors are wide open to every one who has a will to turn to God for forgiveness or for direction. As a mother, she erects no barriers at the door by which to exclude any who desire the strength or the comfort the Church may give. The Church asks only honesty of purpose.

"Men have not always so understood Church affiliation. They have regarded Church allegiance as a profession of superiority in life or character. Men have been honest in their wish to decline an affiliation which implies that they have attained a righteousness which would pass muster at the Church door. Their reluctance to make such a profession is both natural and honorable. If Church membership is a badge of sainthood achieved they will not wear the badge.

"It is unfortunate that such a misconception has had some justification in religious societies. But the Episcopal Church asks for no such profession. As well might a college ask the entering student to profess profound scholarship. The student goes to college not because he has attained scholarship, but because he respects scholarship and would give himself the chance to attain it. The man enters the Church not because he has attained righteousness, but because he respects righteousness and would be within its influence.

"So far from being a profession of superior righteousness, it is a simple desire to grow into the life abundant, that is the inspiring avowal of every one who enters the Church. Let it be clearly understood that on this point the Church asks only honesty of purpose.

"Again, the Episcopal Church teaches the joy of life. Too often has the aspect of Christianity been dismal and gloomy. The Church knows that sorrow and pain and sin are part of humanity's burden, but it knows likewise that the message and power of the Church are directed toward assuaging sorrow, relieving pain, and cleansing lives from sin. The Church's message is joyous. It preaches good tidings. Therefore the attitude of the Church toward men is full of the joy of Christ. Consequently the Church emphasizes those occasions in which natural human joy has its expression. The Church is especially sympathetic and tender toward the young. It tries to fill their lives with joy and happiness.

"And this brings me to the Church's attitude toward amusements and recreation.

"The Church's ideal is to consider the whole of life as the subject of its care. Man is a unit, and all his activities affect his spiritual nature. Every current which sweeps into his life from any source modifies his deeper religious experience. Therefore, the Church is justified in scrutinizing every influence which affects its people.

"One of the most insistent of appeals to all sorts and conditions of men is the attractiveness of amusement. This attractiveness has a sound basis in the real nature of men. Play for the child has been found to be not a mere diversion, but a real necessity for its mental and moral growth. Proper play for the individual, or really, the proper counter-balance for the more serious duties of life, is not mere frivolity but a tonic, a necessary ingredient of life for those who do not despise God's gifts of health and sanity.

"Most opportunities for diversion are not only commercialized but they are not free from objectionable features. Therefore any agency by which proper amusement can be provided under conditions not influenced by commercial considerations, is contributing to the wholesome upbuilding of character.

"The Episcopal Church, acting upon this conviction and with full knowledge of the conditions of modern life, often provides for its people the proper amusements and diversions conducted under careful supervision and with the strict intention of deepening the spiritual nature of those for whom it is caring. Such activities directed in proper channels and diverted from improper ones, have been found to free young people from a certain suspicion of the Church as antagonistic to the simple pleasures of youth. Young men and young women are permitted to meet for social diversions in which a high standard of mutual respect is upheld. The world, itself, recognizes that the normal condition of society is for men and women to meet together and it would be folly to assume that the best ideals of the race are to be attained by preventing such association. Consequently, in their youth there must be an opportunity for young men and women to meet and respect each other. This mutual acquaintance soon brings keen judgment and the faculty of discrimination, and no boy or girl who has normal opportunities for meeting other boys or girls is going to be so quickly deceived as to the real worth of character in another as one who has not had such opportunities. Such acquaintance and companionship are affected by the environment in which it is maintained.

"It must not be supposed that the Church considers this the fulfillment of its mission. It is but one of the attempts of the Church to serve the real needs of the community. The real mission of the Church is never lost sight of, that is, to bring individuals into the Kingdom of God and to make them realize their personal relation to Jesus Christ as their Saviour. The Episcopal Church is not apprehensive of the effect of its social emphasis because it has its foundation most firmly rooted and does not distrust its people. It believes that social service is a natural outcome of its fundamental principles. Its whole structure is comprehensive and not exclusive.

"The Church's message truly presents the

vision of that greater democracy for which the righteous nations of the earth are yearning. It is a democracy whose fundamentals are justice, righteousness and the abundant spirit of service that will secure for the people what no form of economic democracy will ever achieve. For nations seeking national and social salvation from the ills that afflict them, as well as for individuals, Jesus Christ is the Way, the Truth and the Life. The Gospel of Christ is the only national Charter of Liberty that can guarantee national salvation, the only power equal to the task of exalting a nation. The Church presents this Gospel.

"And finally," concluded the Rector, "the Episcopal Church has a supreme confidence in life. Life is God's gift, not His curse. This is God's world, not man's prison. Pain and sacrifice are here, but there are likewise joy and blessing.

"All these considerations appeal to men of today. The Church is slowly but surely bringing the men of today back to the satisfaction, the mental and moral stimulus, the keener valuations and more enduring riches of the Christian life."

CHAPTER XII.

THE APPEAL OF RELIGION TO MEN.

The Rector was poring over a chess problem when the Doctor appeared the following week.

"What!" he cried, "chess? Isn't that rather too secular for a parson?"

"This problem is too tough for any parson," admitted the Rector.

"You can't growl at it as one can at golf," rejoined the Doctor. "You clergy, nowadays, seem more inclined than ever before to take up secular sports."

"What induces you to call sports secular, Doctor?" asked the Rector.

"Well, I rather think of week day pursuits as secular."

"If you mean that secular things are ungodly or unbecoming a religious person, I must disagree with you as to the use of the word. While it is apparent that certain things are sacred, it is not quite so certain that all things not distinctively sacred are secular or ungodly. There are many pursuits that contribute to one's spiritual power. Proper recreation, for example, which keeps the body in good condition and maintains health, may be a real contribution to man's spiritual efficiency."

"I never did quite see the relation between spirituality and ill health," admitted the Doctor.

"There seems to be a popular delusion," said the Rector, "that the religious person is slightly lacking in robustness and vigor and is inclined to a certain mildness in action and thought. It is all nonsense."

"But is there not some trait that marks the godly man?"

"There are several. A real courage in the face of the trials of this world; a responsiveness to the higher calls of duty; a consideration for others which marks the nobility of the gentleman; a sensitiveness to eternal values in life's experiences; and a sense of God's law and love."

"I rather thought the godly man was the man who engaged in church work."

"Church work is merely one expression of man's godliness. You are dragging about a lot of old notions in your head, Doctor," said the Rector, earnestly. "All work has its spiritual aspect. The man who runs a factory or a store, or who works at a desk or at a bench, is as much engaged in processes which have spiritual interpretation as the man who runs a church society. He is engaged in making some material things or in directing some forces which contribute to the sum total of human resources. Ultimately, every human effort is designed to affect the lives of people. An engineer builds a bridge with the expectation that someone will travel over it. Consequently every man who builds honesty into the fabric of his creation, justice into his relations with men both immediate and remote, and uprightness into his affairs, and who emphasizes by his actions and speech the principle that money or gain is not the only, or perhaps the vital part of life's transactions, that man is contributing to the spiritual wealth of the world.

"Your profession, Doctor, and every man's vocation or trade, has in it a large element of ministration to some human need. That is why work is not secular, in the sense of being ungodly, but has some sacred element.

"This attitude toward the world would change our whole conception of life. You find life very interesting, do you not, Doctor?"

"Immensely," asserted the Doctor with vigor. "Every day is a new world."

"In times past there has been an attitude toward the world, especially among religious people, that to me has bordered on superstition. It has been thought that the world was like a quagmire, through which men must struggle as best they could, in order to reach the other shore. A man in it must work, to be sure, but that was but a concession to necessity and part of the hindrance to the religious life. The secular things were thought to delay and obstruct and corrupt the religious nature. Some hymns reflect this attitude. 'I'm but a stranger here, Heaven is my home. Life is a desert drear, Heaven is my home.'"

"I know those hymns," put in the Doctor.

"They are susceptible of a higher meaning, but literally taken they express a feeling that life is a pretty sad affair, and that the world is hopeless. Now to me such a point of view seems utterly lacking in understanding of what the purpose of God is. I can hardly conceive it to be consistent with God's love or mercy or justice, to create a race of men on the earth, and to make them creatures dependent for long years upon the environment and resources of earth, to plant desires and aspirations in their natures, and then to arrange that earthly occupations and earthly activities are entirely destructive of their souls."

"It does seem rather lacking in love," said the Doctor.

THE APPEAL OF RELIGION TO MEN

"I believe quite the contrary to that which I have stated," continued the Rector. "I know that men fall short of perfection, but I believe that the proper use of the world may contribute spiritual fibre, religious content, and moral substance to life. A man may grow in godliness, even though he finds a method of expressing it in so-called secular pursuits and relations.

"And I believe that our Church has this same attitude. It does not look upon your secular pursuit or recreation as a concession to wordly necessity, but as a sphere of action, normal and useful, in which your spiritual nature finds a field of exercise, of discipline, and of growth. I believe that there is many a man, doing fine service in shop and office, who is in a much nobler relation to the will of God than he realizes."

"But some men are far from that ideal, you must admit," urged the Doctor.

"Some men are pure worldlings. They have staked their all on the rewards of time and sense, on material possessions and sensual gratifications. They have not only bartered eternity for a few selfish years, but they have sunk the nobler satisfactions of life for a few worthless toys."

"But the others. Why should they go to church?"

"They should go to church because the Church respects them as men of action, doing useful things, and the Church will give them that appreciation which will keep them steadfast. They should go to church because they there will be constantly reminded that their uprightness and honesty are worth while. Because they will there learn the larger, more lasting and satisfying relations of their lives and actions. Because they will be stimulated to maintain high principles unto the end. Because their own lives will be interpreted to them in the light of God's plan for mankind. Because they will be warned of the dangers that surround them. Because they are God's children and the Church is His household and they are privileged to share in its satisfactions. And because, if they do not, they will soon lose sight of the central fact of Christianity and that is the life, work, and death of Jesus Christ, who reveals God to man."

"But do not many men live lives of usefulness and render great service to mankind without going to church?"

"Yes. But do you not realize that we are living and working together in this world? Such men would be a wonderful stimulus to the usefulness of the Church. The Church needs them.

And inasmuch as the Church is the only organization that, with no thought of material gain, seeks to serve men and to bring the power and presence of God into their lives, it is one of the greatest privileges of earth to share in this labor for the race.

"But even if one is content with a certain high usefulness in his chosen field, there is another phase of the whole matter. The Church has some information for that man which his inner being craves.

"The Church believes that the man wishes to know why the great gift of life was given him, how he may see beyond the affairs of the moment, what is expected of one so richly endowed in mind and heart, what share he has in the improvement of the race, what he must do to enrich his own living, what thoughts he must think in order to understand his own relation to God and the world, what efforts he must make to gain real and durable satisfaction, what he may do to avoid the devastating sins, to whom he may appeal to quiet his conscience, how he may gain comfort in time of loss, how he must estimate necessary sacrifices, what powers he may appropriate to expand life and purpose, what unfading compensations there are for righteous effort and finally what his destiny is to be.

"The Church is the guardian of all this knowledge. Imperfectly as it may teach such truths, nevertheless that truth is its treasure.

"If this treasury of truth is drawn upon, men will enlarge their vision and fortify their lives.

"In this day the world is very attractive and alluring. Never were so many opportunities for interest and pleasure opened to human beings as there are today. Never were so many prizes set for the race. And men are surrendering to their fascination. I do not mean by this that pure worldliness is attracting them; not the flesh-pots and the sensualities and the extravagances. These indeed claim their victims. But men, young and old, are captivated by the possibilities for effort, for growth, for exercise of every capacity in the enchantments of modern progress. The finer elements of manhood are indeed enlisted in the service of the prevailing civilization.

"Science, both pure and applied, is asking of men sacrifices, fidelity, concentration and noble-minded consecration. No saint of any age has exhibited more power for sustained service than some of our scientists working for the amelioration of human ills. And this challenge of nature to discover her truth has sounded in the ears of countless young men who have planned to devote their lives to the pursuit of the mysteries of truth in science.

"Applied science, likewise, has captivated her thousands and has claimed the strength of a whole army of trained workers.

"Industry, likewise, has demanded men of strength and of keen minds. Industry has provided a great quest in which the vitality of manhood may be expended without stint. Industry offers all the fascination which the young man craves, and presents him with a problem which is a challenge to his every capacity.

"These things bring their reward, too. In the end they give him leisure and wealth, and a world to see and enjoy. They give friends, power, and a field of service. They provide outlooks, vistas through which his imagination may project itself to a vision of greater conquests. It is very satisfying.

"The Church dares not underestimate the power of civilization. And the Church must not undervalue or malign it.

"But to such as have found in the world complete satisfaction for every conscious need, for every ambition, for the exercise of every abundance of heart and mind, for the employment of every instinct and tendency to helpfulness, and to such as therefore allow the claims of the

Church to go unheeded, the Church has a particular message.

"The logic of such a position is that some men seem to find the world absolutely satisfactory without God. God may be needed by the masses, as a sort of last resort, but to the capable there is a substitute for God. The weakness of their claim for exemption from the service of God is that they have forgotten the gift of life from God, and the gift of capacity from God. They may indeed rightly claim that they are serving mankind in a large way and cannot be spared to serve in minor parochial affairs, they may indeed claim that they must not be expected to substitute minor social services for major, and that their larger work is more important than serving on committees, but they cannot claim exemption from simple gratitude. No man, who has received the blessing of a well protected and well nourished childhood, would in later years neglect his home. So gratitude, first, prompts successful men, and men doing big things in an efficient way, men under the fascination of large tasks, to render special service to God in His Church.

"And the second consideration is of that personal sort of which it is hard to speak without danger of uttering platitudes and conventional phrases. No man would count a highly successful, interesting and useful career very satisfactory if it alienated him from every simple human companionship and friendship, from the joys of home and family. Men rely upon these things to a remarkable degree. Without family and friends this would be a desolate world. Success would be ashes. Our family ties and friendships endure in trial and in adversity. They warm life and illumine it.

"Yet all earthly ties fade. God alone is the great enduring friendly presence. To be a stranger to Him on earth is to be a stranger to Him forever. Never to think of God, never to serve God, never to worship God, never to share in His effort to make His Kingdom prevail, never to pray to Him, never to acknowledge His presence, never to ask His aid, never to recognize Him, is to reject the one enduring companionship. It is true that failing powers bring feeble desires, and that old age may weaken the sense of spiritual ties, but this is only a passing phase in the life of the spirit. The spirit, renewed, invigorated, will live on. Is the all-loving Father to be a stranger? Loneliness is perhaps one of earth's greatest trials. Can eternal loneliness be what is meant by eternal punishment?

"The Church comes into your life to bring you a knowledge of the presence of God. If one were going to live in a far country, would he not, if opportunity offered, make friends of the King of that country?

"The Church comes into your life to make life more joyous, more free from sin, more contented, more spiritually furnished, more sound in its judgment of things that are worth while. But likewise the Church nourishes that growing union with God through Christ which is man's best heritage and the best compensation for his labors.

"Again, every capable, every useful, every successful man must remember that *noblesse oblige;* that is to say, his very superiority in any realm of action places an additional responsibility upon him. If the emphasis of his life is wrong, his influence is confused and deficient. No matter what his own convictions may be as to the things that are eternal, if his manner of life seems to teach that he believes that man lives by bread alone, he fails to make his greatest contribution to the race. For the capable man must remember that his message to mankind is more effectively uttered by his general manner of life than by his words. It may seem a commonplace saying to you, but a man's recognition of some spiritual and eternal value in living is most apparent when he conforms to a practice which in all the ages has been the expression of man's recognition of God, namely the practice of going to church.

"The best contributions of any man, or of any age, to the life of the people are its spiritual contributions. The people need the spiritual treasures more than they need the comforts of civilization. They need to learn the deep satisfactions of righteousness, truth, honor, and purity, and the terrible penalties of sin. 'The soul that sinneth it shall die.' They need to know and to appreciate to the very depths of their being, the very love of God in those words which will sustain one in every kind of poverty and despair, will stimulate one to remain true and to persevere in every sort of difficulty, those words which have the highest hope in them for the persistent godly man, 'Whatsoever a man sows that shall he also reap.' They are a promise that devotion, devotion to one's simple duties, devotion to one's task, will bring not a reward, in the sense of some prize unrelated to his effort, but a harvest, a fulness of value, for the seed sown, the effort made.

"For if careless men tempt others to rely upon worldly rewards or a satisfaction in possession alone, they are committing men to a fruitless manner of life. Civilization and men's material achievements have as much capacity for evil as they have for good. The great war has shown this. Men have turned the finest achievements of our civilization toward destruction. The genius of our race, the wonderful processes of our day, mechanical, electrical, chemical, have become the agencies of war. With the war has arisen the conviction that war will not cease by reason of any sustained superiority of power in the hands of a group of nations, but war will cease when the hearts of men are changed, when the righteousness prevails which will exalt the nations.

"To fail to contribute to the strength of that organization, the Christian Church, which alone teaches those great ideals, is to fail to give the world the only force which will eliminate evil of all sorts, the social evils, the industrial evils, and the racial cupidities which produce a people, not only bent on war, but determined to involve other and more exalted peoples in its ruins.

"To uphold the Kingdom of God is the surest way to transform the unmoral gains of civilization into an agency of righteousness, justice and peace. And you cannot uphold the Kingdom of

God effectively without upbuilding the Church.

"And again, a fact not to be ignored in this world, is the power of sin. Sins, great and small, destroy their tens of thousands. The Church is the only bulwark erected before the human soul to stay the onrushing tides of sin. For not only does the Church teach, protect, and warn, and rescue, but it has one great function more. It applies to life the forgiveness wrought by Jesus Christ on the Cross for the sins of the world. Man's efforts and God's effort through Christ, blend in the mission of the Church to men. Natural and supernatural agencies contribute to man's salvation.

The Christian Church today is essentially patriotic. In times of peace it has built the foundations of justice, patriotism, righteousness and truth into the fabric of rising manhood. It has exalted honor and sacrifice. In time of war the Church gave of its vital strength to the cause of the nation, and its priests and clergy followed the young manhood of the land to the trenches. The armies became the Church militant sent to far-off lands, but morally equipped, spiritually strengthened, encouraged, approved and blessed by the Church at home. The army fighting for liberty is the Church in action, transforming the will of the Church into deeds: expressing the moral judgments of the Church in smashing blows. And it is preparing to go on with the greater task of preparing the people of the land to be worthy of the liberty for which so many have made the supreme sacrifice. And it is within the Church that they who have been bereft of loved ones, may find the assurance that the dead shall rise to life eternal, shall be known again as on earth. Surely the people crave the comfort and assurance of immortality upon the certainty of which the Church pledges its very existence.

"The Episcopal Church sounds its appeal to men, women, and children, to become part of that great army which sustains the banner and the power of Christ. For centuries the Church has poured forth its treasures, its lives, its sacrifices and efforts, for the good of the people. To-day the Church offers to you the heritage of countless centuries. The Church would place all these things at your service. It would make you share in its riches. Would it not be worth while for you to realize the unselfishness and the value of the Church's effort and to share with the Church in the mightiest crusade that ever inspired men, the triumph in the world, and in your life, of the principles and powers of the Kingdom of God?"